What Are They Saying About the Ministerial Priesthood?

Daniel Donovan

PAULIST PRESS
New York/Mahwah, N.J.

BX
1913
. D66
1992

Library of Congress Cataloging-in-Publication Data

Donovan, Daniel, 1937–
    What are they saying about the ministerial priesthood? / Daniel Donovan.
        p.   cm.
    Includes bibliographical references.
    ISBN 0-8091-3318-0
    1. Pastoral theology—Catholic Church.   2. Catholic Church—Clergy.   I. Title.
    BX1913.D66   1992
    262'.142—dc20   92-11649
                                                        CIP

Published by Paulist Press
997 Macarthur Boulevard
Mahwah, New Jersey 07430

Printed and bound in the
United States of America

Contents

In grateful memory
of the many priests, now dead,
who positively influenced my life,
especially:

Elliott B. Allen, C.S.B.
Michael Cline
John Corrigan
John M. Kelly, C.S.B.
Gerald B. Phelan
Karl Rahner, S.J.

Introduction

Priesthood and ministry have been a focus of concern and debate in the Roman Catholic Church more or less continuously since Vatican II (1962–65). The declining number of priests, changing conditions in the church and in the world, and developments in theology have combined to raise questions about almost every aspect of the traditional understanding and practice of the ministerial priesthood. The media have given prominence to two important issues: celibacy and the ordination of women. Although the latter was not even a question for most Catholics at the time of the council, it has become in some parts of the church one of the most controversial elements of the contemporary discussion.

Sexual and other scandals and a general sense of a problem of morale among priests have led some to conclude that the most pressing problem at the moment is one of spirituality. Given the ecclesiology of Vatican II and the secular nature of modern society, what, such people ask, should the spiritual profile of church leaders be, and how can it best be fostered. Others focus on issues of pastoral ministry, including the need to develop collaborative forms of ministry among priests and with qualified lay persons. Ecumenists, for their part, wonder whether the agreed statements on ministry produced by various bilateral dialogues will lead to anything in practice. Do they, for example, justify a mutual recognition of orders?

As important as such questions and issues are, they do not form the focus of the present book. Its goal is a modest one: to give some sense of recent Roman Catholic theology of the ordained ministry. The topic has presuppositions and implications in areas ranging from christology, pneumatology, and ecclesiology to sacramental and liturgical theology. Theology of ministry, moreover, like all theology, involves methodological options, including decisions about criteria. The fact that the book confines itself to the more strictly theological questions is not to deny the pressing nature of other issues. The focus results partly from the need to make the topic manageable and partly from the author's conviction that agreement about practical matters will require a greater consensus in theology than presently exists.

Given the large number of publications available, choices have had to be made which to some may appear arbitrary. The first two chapters evoke recent formulations of the magisterium beginning with the theology of the presbyterate contained in the documents of Vatican II. The authors treated in subsequent chapters represent a range of views all of which have been important in the ongoing discussion. I have opted to restrict the presentation to a limited number of major figures and works rather than to try for even the appearance of exhaustiveness. Quotations from the documents of Vatican II are, with minor changes, from *The Documents of Vatican II,* ed. W. Abbott (New York: Guild Press, 1966); biblical references are from the *New American Bible with Revised New Testament.*

I have tried to be fair and even sympathetic in the presentation of the different authors, all of whom have something substantial to say. My own experience has been that even when I have disagreed with them I have learned from them.

1
Vatican II: A New Beginning

In the late 1960s there was a widespread belief that priests had been largely forgotten at Vatican II. Its emphasis had been on bishops and on the laity. As far as the post-conciliar period was concerned, the challenge seemed to be to implement collegiality and to facilitate the involvement of all believers in the church's life and mission. As broadly shared, however, as this perception was, the council not only addressed the issue of the ministerial priesthood, but much of what it said marked a shift away from the theological model that had been dominant since the Council of Trent. One of the reasons for this not being immediately evident was that the new insights were only being developed as the council unfolded. The key document, moreover, *Presbyterorum ordinis* (PO), the decree on the ministry and life of priests, received its final form in November 1965, by which time, in the minds of many, the post-conciliar agenda had already been set.

The history of PO, including the changes that its title underwent, indicates something of the shift that was taking place. Originally called *de clericis* (on clerics), it became *de sacerdotibus* (on priests), then *de vita et ministerio sacerdotium* (on the life and ministry of priests), and finally *de presbyterorum ministerio et vita* (on the ministry and life of presbyters). The reversal of the words "ministry" and "life" was significant. The bishops wanted to emphasize that the priesthood is not in the first place a state of life but rather a function, a service, a ministry. The kind of human and spiritual life that priests are called to embrace flows from, and has to be seen in relation to, what they are called to do. Here was a new way of understanding the unity of the priestly life and the distinctive form of its spirituality.

Priest or Presbyter

The other change in the title, that from *sacerdos* to *presbyter*, requires some explanation. The Latin word *sacerdos* and its Greek equivalent *hiereus* are sacral terms. They refer to priests, to those who in the history of religion are usually associated with sacrifices and temples. Such figures were well known in the life of Israel. The great temple of Jerusalem with its extensive and rich sacrificial ritual was presided over by members of the tribe of Levi. In the time of Jesus the priestly caste was made up of the high priest, the priests, and various other functionaries. The Latin word *presbyter*, on the other hand, like its Greek equivalent *presbyteros,* does not have the same sacral overtones. It means an older person or more technically an elder, someone with a certain standing and authority within a particular group or community. Presbyters are not priests. In the history of Israel they appear in a variety of contexts, usually as counselors. By the beginning of the Christian era groups of elders or presbyters exercised a certain administrative responsibility in local synagogues.

In dealing with the ordained ministry, the Council of Trent made the priestly category central. God, it affirmed, had always seen to it that there would be priests. And so, following the pattern of the priesthood of Aaron, Christ at the last supper ordained the apostles priests (*sacerdotes*) and entrusted to them the sacrifice of the eucharist. What Christ initiated continues to be done in the church through the sacrament of ordination.

Although the bishops at Trent called for a renewal of preaching and of pastoral activities, these elements failed to appear in their doctrinal statement. This was partly due to the defensive and polemical nature of the council's task. In regard to the ordained ministry it was instructed by the papal legates not to attempt a full treatment of the topic but simply to affirm those elements of the Catholic tradition which Luther and the other reformers had denied. These included the sacramental character of ordination, the sacrificial nature of the mass, and the priestly understanding of the ministry.

Luther and, even more, Calvin recognized the importance of the ministry, but they related it primarily to preaching and to teaching. When it came to the language of priesthood, Luther pointed to its absence in the New Testament (NT) for community leaders. Hebrews speaks of the priesthood but only in relation to Christ. Other texts evoke the priesthood of all believers. The classic passage to which the reformers appealed here is 1 Peter 2:4–10, a text that is not quoted by Trent.

The renewal of historical and biblical scholarship prior to Vatican II made some Catholics aware of the one-sidedness of Trent's formulations and of the ambiguity of the traditional emphasis given to the priestly category. The need was felt to look at how and why priestly language for the ministry had been introduced and in the light of that to make some judgment about its continuing validity. People also wondered whether, in the polemical response to the reformers, aspects of the Catholic tradition might not have been neglected.

The issue of terminology is not insignificant. It points to deeper realities reflecting fundamentally different theological approaches. For this reason our treatment of Latin documents will use "priest" as a translation of *sacerdos* and the somewhat awkward "presbyter" for its Latin equivalent. This is all the more important as the available English translations of the conciliar documents use "priest" for both Latin words, thus making it all but impossible to understand the nuances of the council's teaching.

Christ's Threefold Office

Central to Vatican II's ecclesiology is its use of the notion of the threefold office or ministry of Christ. He is prophet, priest, and king. The terminology is not always the same, nor is the order of the titles. Teacher is sometimes used for prophet, and pastor or shepherd for king. As applied to Christ the titles are traditional and can be found in various juxtapositions in both the patristic and the medieval periods. It was Calvin, however, who systematized them and made them the key to his soteriology. In the late eighteenth century they were applied by Catholic theologians to office in the church, a practice that was followed by both Pius XI and Pius XII. At the council they are used to give some kind of systematic formulation both to the dignity and role of the laity and to the distinctive nature of the ordained ministry.

There is inevitably something arbitrary about focusing on these three terms. They were not the only categories used in the NT nor are they the only ones available today. Vatican II itself, for example, in its Constitution on the Church in the Modern World speaks repeatedly of Christ as the perfect human, as the one who embodies the ideal of human life.

If the three terms are not the only possible ones, they are also in the conciliar documents not always clearly distinct from one another. Sometimes the word pastor is taken in a broad sense to include preaching and sanctification; at other times it is understood more narrowly as a kind of governing or administrative authority alongside and in addition to sacramental and teaching activities. At other times again, the priestly category is the dominant one and includes the other two. The identification in some texts of sanctification with the priestly function tends to suggest that the ministry of the word and pastoral leadership are without significance in this area, which of course is not the case. Whatever the limitations of the threefold division—and they should always be kept in mind— it remains the primary organizing principle for much of the council's ecclesiology.

In spite of the importance given to the threefold office of Christ, it was inevitable that in certain contexts and from certain perspectives the category of priesthood would dominate. This is particularly true of some of the early documents and especially of the Constitution on the Liturgy, *Sacrosanctum concilium* (SC). There the active role that all are called to play in the liturgy is justified by an appeal to the common priesthood. The presiding function of the bishop is similarly described in priestly terms. Appeal could be made here to texts dating from as early as the late second century. Historically the role played by bishops in the liturgy and especially in the eucharist was a major factor in the increasing application to them in the early centuries of priestly language.

Ministerial and Common Priesthood

The fact that Luther's rejection of the priestly understanding of the ministry was directly coupled with his emphasis on the priesthood of the faithful made a number of bishops at Vatican II hesitant about the council's repeated use of 1 Peter 2:5,9. Although a variety of ways are used to stress the dignity and responsibility of all believers, affirmations about their sharing in the priesthood of Christ carried particular historical and emotional overtones. It was probably for this reason that when the theme of the universal priesthood was first introduced in the Constitution on the Church, *Lumen gentium* (LG), an effort was immediately made to distinguish it from, and to relate it to, the "ministerial or hierarchical priesthood." In the light of the developed theology of PO or even of the formulation in LG 28, the real issue is not relating the two priesthoods but rather understanding the ordained ministry in the whole range of its functions in relation to the broader community of the baptized. That the need was felt in LG 10 to address the issue in terms of priesthood reflects the importance of priestly language in the Catholic tradition. The post-conciliar debates have shown that the concerns were not ungrounded.

Some bishops wanted to distinguish the two priesthoods by calling the one in which all share "metaphorical" or "spiritual" or "initial." The council rejected these efforts as inadequate. It speaks simply of "the common priesthood" and recognizes its "ontological" priority. The phrase points to that being in Christ which makes possible the ethical and religious life of grace. The ministerial or hierarchical priesthood is said to exist to foster and nourish the common priesthood. The language used to described the ordained priesthood in LG 10 is taken from earlier twentieth century popes. "The ministerial priest, by the sacred power he enjoys, molds and rules the priestly people. Acting in the person of Christ, he brings about the eucharistic sacrifice and offers it to God in the name of all the people." While both priesthoods share in the priesthood of Christ, they differ from one another "in essence and not only in degree."

This last phrase, which echoes Pius XII's *Mediator Dei,* was a late addition requested by Paul VI. At the time and since, it has provoked considerable comment. Yves Congar, for example, has written of his initial negative reaction, which upon reflection he felt to be unwarranted. The relation between the two priesthoods is in fact not one of degree. The ordained priest is not a super Christian; the hierarchy is not a hierarchy of grace but of service. The common priesthood and its sacrifice have to do with life. Here there is considerable scope for growth and development. The ministerial priesthood does not fit in at a particular point on the scale of holiness, but is rather of a different order. By definition it is a ministry, a service, through which Christ the one priest continues to sanctify and build up his priestly community.

Taken in isolation LG 10, although it goes beyond Trent in its effort to relate the ministerial priesthood to that of all the faithful, is an inadequate expression of Vatican II's teaching on the ordained ministry. What it affirms is part of that teaching, but to be understood it has to be seen in relation to the more systematic and balanced presentation that the council was still to make. It needs to be understood in relation to the whole of the council's ecclesiology.

Hierarchy as Ministry

Central in the development of that ecclesiology was the decision to insert a chapter on the people of God before the chapter on the hierarchy in LG. Pre-conciliar ecclesiology tended to focus on the visible and institutional aspects of the church. Its dominant model was that of the perfect society. The initial chapter of LG on the mystery of the church tried to root the conciliar reflection in the Trinity and in the story of salvation. Before all else the church is a religious reality comprehensible only in the light of the self-communication of God revealed in Christ and experienced in his Spirit. At the deepest level it is a mystery of communion and community, among believers and with God. To express this the council used the biblical images of the body of Christ, the temple of the Spirit, and, above all, the people of God.

Through faith and baptism all believers are called to participate actively in the life and mission of the church. This is a central theme of the council coming back in such different documents as those on the liturgy, the church, the lay apostolate, and the church in the modern world. The ordained ministry does not exist above or outside this communion, this people, but rather inside it. It exists in order to offer it leadership, to build it up, to serve it in all its members in their efforts to become the kind of persons and community that they are called to be.

Vatican II reflects the rediscovery that was taking place at the time of the biblical roots of the term ministry. In his Latin translation of the NT Jerome had recourse to the word *ministerium* and its cognates for the general NT use of such words as *diakonia* and *diakonos*. When the latter seemed to refer to someone exercising a particular office he translated it as *diaconus*. The language of ministry in a Christian context thus points back to the NT use of *diakonia*. An ordinary Greek word with the meaning of service or even of waiting on table, it took on a special significance in the gospels. In Luke's version of the last supper, for example, Jesus contrasts the attitude of the powerful among the Gentiles to the one that should mark his followers. "The kings of the Gentiles lord it over them and those in authority over them arc addressed as 'Benefactors,' but among you it shall not be so. Rather, let the greatest among you be as the youngest, and the leader as the servant." The model that is offered is Jesus: "I am among you as the one who serves" (Lk 22:25–27). A favorite text of the council in this regard is Mark 10:45: "The Son of Man did not come to be served but to serve and to give his life as a ransom for many."

The conciliar documents appeal to the language of *diakonia* and service especially when the governing or ruling aspect of Christ's threefold office is applied to bishops and presbyters. They are not to dominate over but rather serve and build up the community of faith. *Diakonia* suggests a fundamental attitude for officeholders and even more profoundly points them to the christological basis of their ministry. They are called to identify with and in some way render present the self-giving service of Christ. Put in a slightly different way, Christ continues his ministry in and through them. Theirs is a sacramental identity and function.

Episcopate and Presbyterate

If Vatican II insists upon the necessity of seeing the ordained ministry as existing in and for the community, it also emphasizes its organic nature. It does this first of all by insisting on the sacramental character of the episcopacy. The medieval focus on the power to offer mass as the key to the sacrament of orders made it difficult to understand how the episcopal office could be a sacramental reality. Bishops were thought of as priests with added jurisdiction and authority. The council not only defined the sacramental character of the episcopacy but also made it rather than the priesthood the fundamental category for understanding ordained ministry. Both the episcopate and the presbyterate are, moreover, regarded as collective realities. To be ordained a bishop is to become a member of the college or order of bishops. A central result of the debate about collegiality was the realization that all bishops together, with and under the bishop of Rome, have a responsibility for the universal church. This represents a rediscovery of the early church notion of the *ordo episcoporum.*

Something analogous took place in regard to presbyters. If LG 10 spoke of the priest in the singular, PO consistently uses the plural or the collective. It opts, as already indicated, for the language of presbyter rather than of priest. It speaks of the presbyterate and of the *ordo presbyterorum.* There is no such thing as a free-lance priest. To be ordained a presbyter is to enter into an order of presbyters who with the order of bishops have a responsibility for the universal church. It also implies in most cases the entry into a particular presbyterium, a group of presbyters, diocesan and religious, who are committed to pastoral ministry with and under a diocesan bishop. Like much else in Vatican II's teaching on the ministry, the source here is the early church. The references are to the classic texts of Ignatius of Antioch and the *Apostolic Tradition.* In some instances the presbyterium seems to be restricted to presbyters while in others like LG 28 it clearly includes the bishop. In every case the emphasis is on the communal and collegial nature of the presbyterate.

Several lively debates took place in the discussion of PO. In one case opinion was divided on whether the presentation should focus on the episcopacy and its threefold office in which presbyters participate, or whether it should be focused on the traditional category of the priesthood. PO 2 represents a compromise. In attempting to satisfy both positions, the council had to sacrifice consistency. Having said that the presbyterate participates in the same threefold ministry of Christ as the episcopacy, the text goes on to focus on Christ's priesthood.

If ecclesial office is to be seen in relation to Christ's threefold office, if it represents at various levels a participation in it, then preaching, teaching, sanctification, worship, and pastoral leadership are all of the essence of office. It is therefore confusing to single out one aspect of Christ's office when defining one or other of the ministries. This is exactly what happened historically. The early church emphasized all three offices while the medieval period in its treatment of the presbyterate focused on the language of priesthood. Inevitably the office came to be understood in an increasingly sacerdotal or cultic way. The presbyter is understood as the priest whose main task it is to offer the sacrifice of the mass.

In the Person of Christ

The intent of Vatican II is not to deny this aspect of the presbyterate but to integrate it into a broader and more balanced vision, one that would do justice to preaching, teaching, and pastoral leadership as well as to sacramental activity. The way that was chosen to do this, as already indicated, was to appeal to the threefold office of Christ and to the fact that the episcopate and the presbyterate participate in all aspects of it. This having been affirmed quite clearly in PO 1, it seems confusing if not inconsistent in the following section to focus one-sidedly on Christ's priesthood. While the presbyterate "presupposes the sacraments of Christian initiation, the sacerdotal office (*sacerdotium*) of presbyters is conferred by that special sacrament through which they, by the anointing of the Holy Spirit, are marked with a special character and are so configured to Christ the priest that they can act in the person of Christ the head (*in persona Christi capitis*)" (PO 2).

The idea of the ordained minister acting in the name and in

the person of Christ has long been a part of the Catholic tradition. Coupled with a corresponding reference to the church, it was a central feature of the medieval theology of orders. Although not used at Trent, it became a marked feature of the teaching of twentieth century popes on the ministerial priesthood. In one form or another, and applied to bishops as well as to presbyters, it recurs several times in the documents of Vatican II.

The significance of the reference to Christ the head, especially within a context that speaks of Christ's priesthood, is not immediately evident. In PO 6 Christ's headship seems to be identified with his pastoral office. In LG 13 headship is placed in apposition to the threefold office as in some sense summing up and including all its aspects. In PO 12 presbyters are said to be "configured to Christ the priest so that as ministers of the head and co-workers of the episcopal order they can build up and establish his whole body which is the church." Here we seem to have come full circle. The basic fact about presbyteral ordination is that it introduces people to an order of ministry the very nature of which is to be cooperators with bishops in the whole breadth of episcopal responsibilities. The reference to Christ the head must be to the risen Christ who continues to exercise through various church ministries his teaching, sanctifying and pastoral functions.

From a certain perspective the ministry rises up out of the church even as it is called to serve it. In many of their actions, the ordained act in the name of the community. The Catholic understanding of office, however, includes a second affirmation. Office-holders act both in the name of the church and in the name of Christ. The capacity to do the latter is understood as rooted in the apostolic office and to be communicated by sacramental ordination. The fact that ministers, especially in the eucharist but also analogously in other aspects of their functioning, are seen to represent Christ, to be "living instruments" of his continuing activity, underlines the radical dependence of the church on the risen Lord. Christ is both immanent to the church and over against it. This duality is part of the church's present historical condition; it is something that will only be overcome when it is brought to its fulfillment. The Catholic tradition sees this continuing activity of

Christ in word, liturgy, and pastoral leadership as tied up, although not exclusively, with the ordained ministry.

An Evangelical Emphasis

Much of the ecclesiological renewal that made Vatican II possible took place in France immediately before and after the Second World War. It was largely inspired by, and tried to contribute to, renewal efforts in liturgy and pastoral practice. The development of Catholic Action and of such apostolic efforts as the *Mission de France* and the worker priests grew out of a growing awareness that in spite of its rich Catholic history, France had become a *pays de mission,* a missionary territory. This awareness and the initiatives undertaken to respond to it seemed to call for a rethinking of the nature of the ministerial priesthood. Coming out of this background many French bishops argued at the council for a theology of the priest that would be more evangelical and missionary than cultic. The need, they believed, was for priests who would see their first task as that of preaching the gospel to non-believers.

Although the council's presentation of both the episcopacy and the presbyterate was markedly influenced by the situation and theology of the patristic church, the efforts of the French and other bishops were not in vain. The documents do reflect a missionary perspective. They move away from a narrowly cultic understanding of the ministry and emphasize the importance of preaching.

It is said that among the functions of bishops preaching holds an eminent place (LG 25). In their case as in that of presbyters, their sharing in the teaching and prophetic functions of Christ is listed before their priestly and leadership responsibilities. This priority makes particular sense from a missionary perspective. Until there is faith there can be no sacramental life, and until the gospel is preached there can be no explicit faith. "Presbyters, as co-workers with their bishops, have as their primary duty the proclamation of the gospel of God to all." By so doing they fulfill the missionary mandate of Christ (Mk 16:15) (PO 4). The ministry of the word takes many forms including catechetics, teaching, and liturgical preaching. This latter is to be exercised not only in the eucharist, but in all the sacraments, "for these are sacraments of faith, and faith is born of the word and nourished by it."

A Spiritual Sacrifice

Beyond these general affirmations about the importance of preaching and evangelization, PO 2 tries to show how a properly Christian understanding of cult necessarily includes a ministry of the word. Yves Congar was a member of the subcommittee which wrote this section. His theology and concerns are clearly visible in it. Appeal is made to the NT and to its use of priestly and sacrificial categories. Paul as well as others adopted and developed a tendency that was already noticeable in the prophets and among the psalmists to use the language of sacrifice for a life pleasing to God. What God wants, Psalm 51 affirms, is not holocausts but a contrite and humbled heart. Paul encourages the Romans to offer their bodies, their very selves, as a sacrifice holy and pleasing to God (Rom 12:1).

For Christians the key to this transformation, this personalization, of the notion of sacrifice is Christ himself. The interpretation of his life and above all of his death as a sacrifice is a recognition that through his faith and self-giving love he both offered perfect worship to God and became the instrument of salvation. Life in Christ, a life of discipleship made possible by the gift of his Spirit, is the sacrifice that God now demands of us. This sacrifice corresponds to our common priesthood. The council brings Romans 16:15 in relation to this sacrifice. Paul describes his service of the gospel as a sacral, perhaps even as a priestly act. By his preaching he has helped people to live the kind of life which is the perfect sacrifice.

The point that the document is trying to make here is that evangelization and indeed anything that the ordained minister does which contributes to the building up of the Christian life of others are cultic acts. The text does not simply juxtapose priestly with prophetic and pastoral activity, but seeks to broaden the meaning of cultic and sacerdotal language until it includes every aspect of the presbyter's life. If the deep meaning of sacrifice and priesthood has to do with the quality of the life of believers, then all pastoral activity that serves and fosters it has a priestly dimension. When this activity is performed by ordained ministers in the name and in the person of Christ, then, no matter what it is, it pertains to the ministerial priesthood as such.

The category of priesthood has created a problem for modern Roman Catholics. Given its all but total absence from NT understandings of the ministry, some have simply rejected it. Others have tried to maintain it while balancing it by evoking the threefold office of Christ and by insisting on the importance of preaching and other forms of pastoral activity. The present text appeals to a distinctively NT understanding of priesthood and sacrifice. It is an attempt that few seem to have understood or to have developed in any significant way in the post-conciliar period.

Bishops and Presbyters

Vatican II's emphasis on the episcopate and its understanding of the presbyterate in relation to it led on occasion to some rather surprising formulations. It is said, for example, that presbyters in some sense (*quodammodo*) render the bishop present in the local community (LG 28; PO 5). Sharing as presbyters do in the grace of the episcopal office (LG 41), the efficacy of their ministry as well as their holiness depends to a considerable degree on a willing and genuine cooperation with the bishop. The council repeatedly affirms that presbyters by definition are helpers and collaborators of the episcopal order. If this implies that bishops ought to take their advice seriously, it also calls for obedience and deference on the part of presbyters. The language used in describing the relation between the bishop and his presbyters is sometimes paternalistic.

The emphasis on the bishop provoked a double reaction within the council. The German and Scandinavian hierarchies, in particular, were anxious to mitigate any paternalism. In both LG and *Christus Dominus* (CD), the pastoral decree on the bishop's office, bishops are admonished to treat presbyters as "sons and friends." In PO 7 "sons" becomes "brothers." More significant was the reaction against the tendency to interpose the bishop between the presbyter and Christ. If a person becomes a presbyter through ordination by a bishop, and if the exercise of the office demands "hierarchical communion" with the local ordinary, the presbyter, nonetheless, shares in the consecration and mission of Christ. He is configured to Christ, prophet, priest and shepherd, so that in his ministry he "represents the person of Christ himself (*ipsius Christi personam gerat*)" (PO 12). Presbyters are "living instruments" of the risen Christ who through them continues his own teaching and sanctifying ministry.

A Ministerial Spirituality

Although it is beyond our scope to go into the details of what the council had to say about presbyteral spirituality, it is significant to note that in spite of a certain opposition, it sought its unifying principle in the ministry itself. Because presbyters are called to serve Christ's continuing pastoral concern for his people, their life is to be distinguished by what is called "pastoral charity" (PO 14). Not inconsistently it is the same virtue that CD most pressingly demands of bishops.

The idea of a spirituality rooted in the pastoral ministry marks a shift from pre-conciliar emphases. The French school of spirituality tended to see the priest as a man set apart, *homo segregatus*, dedicated in a special way to a life of prayer and contemplation. The heart of his spiritual life was the sacrifice of the mass. The priest's task is to share in Christ's sacrifice by a life of prayer and self-denial. By that fact he contributes to the building up of the church. This enormously influential spirituality was almost entirely conceived apart from any actual involvement in the pastoral ministry. It could be embraced by monk, religious, or parish priest.

The traditional approach is evoked and transformed in PO 3. The section begins with an obvious paraphrase of Hebrews 5:1, a favorite text in earlier papal documents as well as on ordination cards. That the reference was made at all was a concession to one side in the ongoing debate. What traditionally was suggested by the quotation, however, is undermined by the way it is used. The subject of the sentence is not priest in the singular but presbyters in the plural. More importantly its meaning is modified by being juxtaposed to the broader message of Hebrews. More than any other NT document Hebrews insists on the humanity of Jesus. He is truly our brother, like us in all things but sin. In other words, the text cannot be used as a basis for an understanding of ministry that would be narrowly cultic or that would separate presbyters from their people.

The paragraph goes on to evoke another classic text of the traditional spirituality, the *homo segregatus* theme of Romans 1:1. This, however, as the council argues, does not mean "separated." Paul and presbyters after him are indeed "set apart," but within the people of God and for a particular task. It is said that presbyters "cannot be ministers to Christ unless they are witnesses and dispensers of a life other than this earthly one. But they cannot be of service to people if they remain strangers to their life and condition" (PO 3). The section ends with a reference to their pastoral responsibilities and to the human and Christian virtues without which they will not be able to fulfill them.

An attempt like this to ground the spirituality of the presbyterate in its actual ministry underlines that it is not primarily a state of life. Although rooted in the reality of grace and demanding a life of holiness, it is by definition ordered to activity on behalf of others. The basic thrust of the council goes beyond any simplistic opposition between ontological and functional understandings of the ministry.

The Role of the Laity

If its theology of the episcopacy influenced the council's treatment of the presbyterate, so too did its approach to the laity. The very nature of the presbyteral office as a pastoral ministry in and to the church implies that any significant shift in ecclesiology or church practice will necessarily entail repercussions for the ministry and life of presbyters. This is certainly the case at Vatican II.

Space and the focus of the present book do not allow any detailed review of what the council says about the laity. Let it simply be recalled that they are no longer to be defined negatively as the non-ordained, nor are they to be seen as passive objects of the clergy's ministrations. The church is a community in which all share in a common dignity and vocation. Through faith and baptism all receive gifts of the Spirit and all are called to become actively involved in building up the church and serving its mission. The ordained ministry exists within the church in order to serve and foster the faith and life of all its members. It will only be able to do so to the extent that it recognizes and respects the radical equality and dignity of everyone (LG 32) and calls forth their gifts and talents so that they too can be put at the service of the community as a whole.

The council juxtaposes two different kinds of affirmations about the church. Some see them as almost contradictory or at least as unintegrated. It is said, for example, that the liturgy is both "hierarchical" and "communitarian." The same two terms apply to the council's ecclesiology. The new emphasis is clearly on the community dimension, on the gifts and responsibilities that all believers have in common. At the same time the traditional Catholic understanding of the hierarchy as belonging to the church by divine institution is not denied. The bishops are careful to avoid historical affirmations about the details of the development of various offices in the early church, but they do maintain that ecclesial office as such continues and is rooted in the apostolic ministry which itself was called into existence by the express will of Christ and by the gift of the Pentecostal Spirit. What is essential is that office not be defined in opposition to, or in separation from, the spiritual reality of the community. The ordained are not the only active agents of the church's life and mission. If, in fact, they are going to be able to fulfill their tasks, it will only be in the closest collaboration with the whole body of the faithful (LG 31ff; PO 9).

Change and Continuity

The reintegration of pastoral responsibilities into the definition of the presbyterate is, perhaps, the key to Vatican II's advance beyond the post-Tridentine tradition. Given the developments of medieval theology, Trent, as aware as it was of the need for a renewal of the pastoral life of the church, focused its dogmatic formulation on the sacrifice of the mass and on the power that the priest receives through ordination to offer it. A spirituality was subsequently developed to correspond to this focus, and with it the fundamental identity of the modern Catholic priest was determined.

In its desire to emphasize continuity in the midst of development, Vatican II quotes Trent in a key passage (PO 2) and in the end remains inconsistent in its use of priestly language. A striking example of the latter phenomenon is the contrast between the introductory paragraphs of PO and the same paragraphs in the decree on the training of priests (*Optatum totius*). The language of the former is consistently presbyteral, while that of the latter is sacerdotal. The most widely used English translations employ variations of "priest" in every case. The inconsistency probably reflects the difference in the committees that wrote the documents as well as the fact that the theology underlying PO was not embraced by everyone.

The issue of continuity and change is reflected in the treatment of the eucharist. There can be no doubt that Vatican II continued to see it as the font and center of church life. The key paragraph, for example, in PO on the nature of the presbyterate culminates with a reference to it. The eucharist, however, is understood here not as the private mass of the priest but as the eucharist of the community. It involves both word and sacrament. All are called to participate actively in it and, above all, to bring to it their lives of faith and love in order to join them to the self-offering of Christ. The eucharist is thus inseparable from all the institutions and activities that constitute the life of a local church.

The obvious emphasis given by Vatican II to the pastoral dimension of ordained ministry including that of the presbyterate raises questions for the self-understanding of priests with little or no pastoral involvement. The operative model at the council is clearly secular priests and religious involved in diocesan ministry. Consciously or not, this option was reinforced by the influence patristic forms of ministry had on conciliar formulations.

Although there is room for a variety of concrete ministries, there is only one presbyterate. To be ordained a presbyter is to accept a responsibility of some form of pastoral leadership in and to the church. It involves a range of tasks including preaching and teaching as well as liturgical and ritual functions. It is to be exercised in collaboration with other presbyters and in most cases with and under the direction of a local bishop. As a ministry in the church it can only be exercised as it should be in close cooperation with all members of the community. The model whom the council repeatedly presents to bishops and presbyters alike is Christ, the good shepherd, the one who came not to be served but to serve and to give his life for the many.

2
The Magisterium Since the Council

The post-conciliar period has been marked by a great deal of turmoil in regard to the ministerial priesthood. By the late 1960s in many countries it already seemed to be in a state of crisis. Vocations dropped, some priests left the active ministry, while many others underwent what at the time was referred to as an identity crisis, a profound self-questioning involving both personal and theological elements. The theological questioning became, if anything, more intense and more radical in the course of the 1970s and the 1980s. Such developments could not help but provoke a reaction on the part of the magisterium. The present chapter will consider two moments in this reaction, the work of the 1971 synod of bishops and the contribution of John Paul II.

The 1971 Synod

The bishops at their meeting in Rome in 1971 issued a document entitled "On the Ministerial Priesthood" (MP) in which they attempted to address the malaise by reaffirming what they called "some principles of the church's teaching on the ministerial priesthood which are at present more urgent, together with some guidelines for pastoral practice" (MP intro, 7).[1]

Among the factors influencing the situation, the bishops underlined the impact of the rediscovery by Vatican II of the significance

of human history for an understanding of salvation. It had occa-
sioned doubts among some priests about the place of sacrament and
cult and about the value of a life not immersed in the struggle for
justice. The synod itself had taken the question of justice seriously
and had published a document on it in which among other things it
affirmed that "action on behalf of justice and participation in the
transformation of the world fully appear to us as a constitutive
dimension of the gospel." In MP it turned to address some of the
problems this new emphasis was raising for the presbyteral ministry.

The synod attributes another set of problems to a one-sided
enthusiasm in the post-conciliar period for the "common priesthood of the faithful." As positive as the renewed emphasis on this
teaching is, it "gives rise, as by a swing of the pendulum, to certain
questions which seem to obscure the position of the priestly ministry in the church." People are asking: "Does the priestly ministry
have any specific nature? . . . Is the priesthood incapable of being
lost? . . . Would it not be enough to have for the service of the
Christian communities presidents designated for the preservation
of the common good, without sacramental ordination, and exercising their office for a fixed period?" (MP intro, 4) Not surprisingly
these questions as well as other factors raised the issue of celibacy
which, as it turned out, was a major focus of the synod's debates.

The Language of Priesthood

The title of the document as well as the texts already quoted
suggests that the synod failed to understand or to take seriously the
considerable effort made at Vatican II and especially in PO in
regard to terminology. The words *sacerdos* and *presbyter* are used
almost interchangeably. The sacerdotal language sometimes refers
to bishops and presbyters together but more often just to the latter. The title of the second part, *Directoriae rationes quoad vitam et
ministerium sacerdotis,* guidelines for the life and ministry of the
priest, seems an all but deliberate repudiation of the development
at Vatican II which finally led to the formulation, *de presbyterorum
ministerio et vita.*

The phrase, the ministerial priesthood, by itself seems to
make the priestly category again the central if not exclusive one for

understanding the ordained ministry. The breadth of the threefold office and especially the focus on the pastoral as a unifying factor for the ordained ministry disappear. The situation becomes more confused when "ministerial priesthood" is used interchangeably with "the priestly ministry." For all its narrowness the first formulation at least suggests that the priesthood is a larger reality which includes both the priesthood of Christ and that of the community and that the priestly role of the ordained in relation to it is a ministerial one. The second formulation tends to restrict the priestly category to the ordained.

Confusing the issue still further, the bishops affirm that when "we speak of the priesthood of Christ, we should have before our eyes a unique, incomparable reality, which includes the prophetic and royal office of the Incarnate Word of God" (MP I, 1). The desire to broaden the meaning of priesthood is a positive one. In practice, however, it cannot help but lead to a use of sacerdotal language in which the prophetic and the pastoral dimensions of office fade into the background. The shift in language from PO seems to represent a response to what were perceived as secularizing trends in the post-conciliar church. It may also have been thought that a strong emphasis on the priestly category was required to counterbalance the importance being given to the common priesthood of the faithful.

In spite of the priestly language, the synod clearly did not want to restrict priestly activity to the cultic sphere. It cites and reinforces the emphasis of Vatican II on preaching and on evangelization. But even here, one can sense that the bishops are reacting against a tendency to downplay the sacraments in favor of the word. "The ministry of the word, if rightly understood, leads to the sacraments and to the Christian life, as it is practiced in the visible community of the church and of the world" (II,I,1b).

The basic Christian ministry is said to be that of the apostles. "An apostle and a community of faithful united with one another by a mutual link under Christ as head and the influence of his Spirit belong to the original inalienable structure of the church" (I,4). In a formula that is more nuanced than that of Vatican II, it is said that "the powers entrusted to the apostle for the churches were handed on to others insofar as they were communicable." The

result is the "essential structure of the church—consisting of a
flock and of pastors appointed for this purpose. . . . Precisely as a
result of this structure, the church can never remain closed in on
herself and is always subject to Christ as her origin and head." The
text then goes on to interpret this fundamentally pastoral office in
terms of priesthood. "The priestly ministry of the NT, which continues Christ's function as mediator . . . alone perpetuates the essential work of the apostles." (The word "alone" does not occur in the
Latin!) The bishops then list a number of pastoral activities: preaching, community development and leadership, remitting sins and
the presiding at the eucharist. In all these things, it is said that the
ministry "makes Christ, the head of the community, present in the
exercise of his work of redeeming humankind and of glorifying
God perfectly" (I,4). While the summary of the content of the
ministry reflects the teaching of Vatican II, the language used to
describe it falls behind the council in its lack of nuance.

The Sacramental Character

The phenomenon of priests leaving the ministry raised questions about the traditional teaching on the permanence of the presbyteral office. In the popular mind this had been regularly expressed in priestly terms borrowed from Hebrews: "You are a
priest forever according to the order of Melchizedek." The synod's
brief treatment of the topic uses the same kind of argument especially in its reference to configuration with Christ the priest, but it
goes beyond it in its appeal to the NT notion of *exousia* (power or
authority) and to the Pauline idea of being an ambassador for
Christ in the work of reconciliation. "By the laying on of hands
there is communicated a gift of the Holy Spirit which cannot be
lost." This is described as a "teaching of the faith" and identified
with what "in the church's tradition [is called] the priestly character." The document interprets this as a sign of the irrevocable
nature of God's gifts to the church, "a pledge of the salvific presence of Christ" (I,5). The reference to the Holy Spirit in this
context is echoed in other places in the document and suggests a
desire to balance the council's more christological emphasis. The
conclusion describes priests as "exercising the ministry of the Spirit

(cf. 2 Cor 3:4–12) in the midst of the communion of the entire church."

The section on the character contains no reference to the idea of acting "in the person of Christ." The phrase, however, is used elsewhere in regard to the eucharist. There the priest presides over the "sacrificial banquet" "in the person of Christ." This sense of the priest making Christ present in the community comes back in a number of contexts. His is the key ministry without which the church "cannot have final certainty of her fidelity and of her visible continuity" (I,4).

Although the document has brief references to the dignity of all believers, the preoccupation is more with what distinguishes the ordained from the community than with what relates them to it. The synod attempts to respond to the growing identity problem of priests by recalling their traditional responsibilities in regard to word and sacrament and by underlining the uniqueness of the gifts that are theirs through ordination. It stresses their special relationship with Christ the head of the church. The ordained stand, as it were, on the side of Christ over against the community, to which, however, they are sent and in which they play an indispensable role. In comparison with PO, the emphasis is more on priestly life and identity than on the ministry, and more on priesthood than on the threefold and at the same time predominantly pastoral office of the bishop in which presbyters share.

John Paul II

A concern for priests and for their identity and ministry has been a central feature of the papacy under John Paul II. He has touched on the theme of the ministerial priesthood on literally hundreds of occasions, including the talks given to groups of priests in the course of his trips and his Holy Thursday letters. The present brief overview of his thought will be based largely on the letters. Given the complex process that the speeches for the trips go through in the course of their composition, it seems evident that his more personal and spontaneous views are to be found in the Holy Thursday reflections and meditations.[2]

The pope has indicated that the letters were largely stimulated by his sense of the crisis among priests. He speaks of problems of numbers, of age, and even of quality. More significantly he indicates certain developments such as secularization or the one-sided focusing on the temporal, which have tended to undermine priests' sense of identity. He particularly laments tendencies to interpret Vatican II's call for aggiornamento in terms of a breaking down of the differences between the ordained and the laity.

The letters are marked by an exhortatory and an encouraging tone. The pope wants to strengthen priests in their sense of vocation and to stimulate them to renew their commitment. In order to do this he spells out the basic nature of their office, confusion about which, he believes, is at the heart of the crisis. Between the 1979 letter and the more recent ones there are certain shifts of emphasis. The 1987 synod on the laity, for example, has had an influence on the way that the pope articulates the relation between the ordained and the community. For all the differences, however, there are considerable continuities. It is these that I will stress, even while indicating what seem to be developments.

A Priestly Office

The most striking thing about the letters, especially when they are compared with the documents of Vatican II, is the dominant place they give to the category of priesthood. The history of the title of PO was symptomatic of an effort at the council not to deny the priestly aspect of the ordained ministry, but to integrate it into the threefold ministry of Christ and to see the presbyteral office as a sharing in the whole range of episcopal responsibilities. The pope's emphasis on the priesthood is reinforced by his appeal to the Tridentine notion of the institution of the priesthood by Christ at the last supper. The letters refer repeatedly to Holy Thursday as the "feast of priests" or "the birthday of the priesthood."

The emphasis on the priesthood is clearly intentional. In some of the letters the words *sacerdos, sacerdotium,* and *sacerdotalis* come back in almost every paragraph. Reference is made to such things as "priestly life," "priestly ministry," "priestly vocation," "priestly existence," "priestly personality," "priestly consciousness," etc. The phrase "priestly community" seems on some occasions to be a substitute for presbyterium. The relatively brief 1987 letter uses *sacerdotium* seventeen times, *sacerdos* twelve times, *sacerdotalis* fourteen times, *presbyteri* twice and *presbyteratus* once.

Although references are made to the documents of Vatican II and, for example, to what it has to say about the priesthood of the faithful, the overall presentation is more reminiscent of earlier papal encyclicals and of the image of the priest in the French school of spirituality. The presbyter is above all a priest. Through the sacrament of ordination, regularly referred to as the sacrament of the priesthood, the priest shares in a unique way in the priesthood of Christ. The sacrament "imprints on [the priest's] soul the mark of an indelible character" (1979,7) in virtue of which he is able to offer the sacrifice of the eucharist and to forgive sins.

In a rather dramatic passage, the pope evokes a community of believers long deprived of a priest. "And sometimes it happens that they meet in an abandoned shrine and place on the altar a stole . . . and recite all the prayers of the eucharistic liturgy; and then, at the moment that corresponds to the transubstantiation, a deep silence comes down upon them, a silence sometimes broken by a sob . . . so ardently do they desire to hear the words that only the lips of a priest can efficaciously utter. . . . So if one of you doubts the meaning of his priesthood, or if he thinks it is 'socially' fruitless or useless, reflect on this" (1979,10).

In the 1979 letter reference is made to LG and to PO but only LG 10 is quoted. The pope calls it "this classical conciliar text, which expresses the basic truths of [the priests'] vocation in the church" (1979,3). It asserts among other things that the "common priesthood" and the "ministerial or hierarchical priesthood" "differ essentially and not only in degree." The priest, it says, acting "in the person of Christ . . . effects the eucharistic sacrifice and offers it to God in the name of all the people." The phrase about the two priesthoods differing "essentially and not only in degree" comes back four times in the 1979 letter. The other phrase, *in persona Christi,* occurs three times in that letter and then periodically throughout the series (1980,8; 1988,1,2,6; 1989,8; 1990).

Although the notion of acting in the person of Christ could well be applied to all aspects of Christ's threefold ministry, the pope prefers to relate it to the priesthood of Christ and to see it as primarily exercised in the eucharist. The emphasis on the priesthood and the eucharist is accompanied by an emphasis on the sacred and on its importance within the Christian dispensation. Here the pope is reacting against the process of secularization in western culture and against corresponding tendencies in the church to laicize or undermine the sacred character of the ordained.

Vatican II and the synod of 1971 spoke of the priesthood of the ordained as "hierarchical or ministerial." The latter term, according to the pope, points to the fact that it offers a "service in relation to the community of believers." The term, however, is open to misunderstanding. The ministerial priesthood "does not take its origin from the community, as though it were the community that 'called' or 'delegated.' The sacramental priesthood is truly a gift for the community and comes from Christ himself, from the fullness of his priesthood" (1979,4).

The 1989 and 1990 letters are marked by a greater preoccupation with the relation between the ministerial priesthood and the priesthood of the faithful. The ordained receive their priestly vocation within the priestly people of God. Both share in the same priesthood of Christ although in different ways. The 1987 synod and the subsequent papal document on the laity, *Christifideles laici,* have emphasized again the positive role that all are called to play in the life of the church. What is required, however, is not a "clericalizing" of the laity, any more than a "laicizing" of the clergy. "The church develops organically according to the principle of the multiplicity and diversity of 'gifts' " (1989,4).

The Curé of Ars

The letters all have a pastoral emphasis, although it is perhaps significant that like the 1971 synod and unlike Vatican II the pope consistently follows the order "priestly life and ministry" and not the reverse. If the priesthood is a ministry in the church, the pope nonetheless focuses in the first place on priestly identity, ready as it were once this is clarified to insist on tireless and dedicated pastoral activity. The 1986 letter offers the Curé of Ars as a particularly relevant model of priestly ministry. Ours is an age of "growing secularization," a time "when often in the pastoral ministry there is a too exclusive concern for the social aspect, for temporal aims," when "the identity of the priesthood," especially "its vertical dimension," is under attack (1986,2). In such an age the radically supernatural nature of the ministry of Jean Marie Vianney suggests what could be a balance. He was a "matchless pastor, who illustrates both the fullest realization of the priestly ministry and the holiness of the ministry" (1986,2). His life was entirely given over to catechesis, confession, and the eucharist. The pope asks whether we should not "see here, today also, the three objectives of the priest's pastoral service" (1986,6).

This same letter says that Vatican II "has felicitously placed the priest's consecration within the framework of his pastoral mission" (1986,4). As often as the pope refers to Christ as the good shepherd or as often as he evokes the pastoral office of the ordained ministry, one has the impression that the mission aspect is subordinate to the priesthood and not vice versa. In the 1979 letter the good shepherd's laying down of his life for the sheep is said to "refer to the sacrifice of the cross, to the definitive act of Christ's priesthood" (1979,5). Here the priesthood seems to be the key to the "triple dimension of Christ's service and mission," even as it is of the ministry of the ordained. And yet the ministerial priesthood remains a pastoral priesthood at the heart of which is a profound "solicitude for the salvation of our neighbor."

The pastoral activity upon which the pope insists, as the example of the Curé of Ars would suggest, is focused primarily on individuals, on "the direction of souls." In order to do this effectively one has to be with people but one must always be with them "as a priest." Lay Christians are called to work in and to transform the temporal sphere. "But the service of the priest belongs to another order. He is ordained to act in the name of Christ the head, to bring people into the new life made accessible by Christ, to dispense to them the mysteries. . . . Attempts to make the priest more like the laity are damaging to the church. . . . He is the witness and dispenser of a life other than earthly life. It is essential to the church that the identity of the priest be safeguarded, with its vertical dimension" (1986,10).

The pope offers not only a high theology of the priesthood but also an heroic model of priestly holiness. Because they share in Christ's priesthood, priests are called in a special way to intimacy with him. The statement of Jesus to his disciples in John 15:15 that they are no longer servants but friends applies particularly to priests (1990,2). They are called to give themselves "totally to Christ" (1982, intro). They are to identify with him especially in his suffering and death. "In the priest Christ relives his passion for the sake of souls" (1986,11). To celebrate the eucharist is to "stand each day on Golgotha" (1988,2). Everything about the priest comes back to the eucharist. It is "the principal and central *raison d'être* of the sacrament of the priesthood, which effectively came into being at the moment of the institution of the eucharist and together with it" (1980,2).

The letters nowhere deal with the difficulty that arises for a Catholic theology of the ministerial priesthood from the absence of the priestly category in the NT's treatment of ministry. The pope follows Trent in his reading of the significance of the last supper. In the command to "do this in memory of me," Jesus instituted the apostles priests.

The pope considers the letter to the Hebrews "a fundamental text for knowledge" of the ministerial priesthood (1987,3). He cites Hebrews 5:1 on a number of occasions, applying it in turn to Christ, the whole community, and to those who have received "the sacrament of the priesthood" (1979,3; 1989,3,4). Perhaps most striking is the application to priests of Hebrews 5:6: "You are a priest forever according to the order of Melchizedek." The pope reads this as a reference to the "indelible seal" imprinted on the soul of the priest on the day of his ordination (1990,1). Perhaps the favorite NT text of the pope for the ministerial priesthood is 1 Corinthians 4:1: "People should regard us as servants of Christ and stewards of the mysteries of God." He quotes it on a number of occasions and evokes it on many others. It expresses his christocentric view of the ministry even as it clearly implies pastoral responsibilities. Although almost entirely absent from the documents of Vatican II, it was quoted thirteen times in papal encyclicals on the priesthood from Pius X to John XXIII.

Differing Theological Emphases

The debates at, and to some degree the documents of, Vatican II reflected a certain division among the bishops in regard to the emphasis they wanted to give to the ordained ministry. Some preferred the more traditional approach with its focus on the eucharist and on priestly language. Others stressed evangelical and missionary aspects and interpreted both the presbyterate and the episcopate in relation to the threefold office of Christ. Although the second approach denied neither the importance of the eucharist nor the reality of a priestly dimension to the ministry, it did modify their significance by situating them in a different context.

Catholic contributions to ecumenical dialogues as well as efforts at church renewal after the council tended to appeal to the pastoral dimension of the ministry and to break down what was thought to be an excessive separation of the priest from the life and situation of the people he was called to serve. These efforts were sometimes perceived as undermining the sacral character of the priesthood and reducing the priest both theologically and sociologically to the state of the laity. It is against such tendencies that John Paul II has reacted in his ministry and in his writings.

For the pope, the presbyter is above all a priest. By ordination and the character it imprints he shares in a distinctive way in the priesthood of Christ. Endowed with the sacred power to offer the eucharist and to forgive sins he is able to act *in persona Christi.* As much as his ministry is a service to others, as much as he is called to exercise a pastoral role in the community of faith, his priesthood sets him apart and demands of him a heroic effort to identify with Christ the priest and good shepherd who laid down his life for his flock.

The pope's view of the priesthood is christocentric. He understands priests as above all empowered to act in the name and in the person of the risen Christ. Emphasizing as he does the transcendence of Christ to the church, the pope tends to see the priest as separated from and acting upon the community of faith. A good deal of post-conciliar theology, on the other hand, has emphasized the ecclesiological and pneumatological dimensions of the ministry and has thought of Christ as primarily present within the church.

From this perspective the minister is seen more as acting in the person of the church or, if in the person of Christ, then in relation to what Augustine called the total Christ, that is Christ and his ecclesial body. Some of the implications of these different emphases will become evident in what follows.

3
Y. Congar: The Ecclesial Dimension of Ministry

By any reckoning Yves Congar is one of the major Roman Catholic theologians of the twentieth century. A French Dominican, he committed himself at the time of his ordination in 1929 to the service of ecumenism. It was a daring and far-sighted choice. From the beginning his ecumenical concerns were complemented and reinforced by a desire to contribute to the renewal of Catholic ecclesiology. His chosen fields of interest inevitably made Congar a central figure in the renewal efforts that led up to Vatican II. He was named an expert to the council's theological commission by John XXIII and in that capacity was able to influence several of its texts, including those on the church, the presbyterate, and the missions. He was particularly concerned about the initial failure of the council to address issues related to the ministerial priesthood and was a key figure in the writing of the more theological paragraphs of *Presbyterorum ordinis*. He said later that his involvement in the drafting of that document was one of the great joys of his life.

Congar's bibliography is enormous. It includes many historical as well as theological books and articles. In regard to the ordained ministry, he himself has referred on several occasions to changes and developments in his position. To read his many studies and statements on the topic from the 1930s to the late 1980s is to become aware of just how much has taken place in both theology and the life of the church during that period and to recognize the significant role that Congar played in it.[1]

From the outset, the primary reality for Congar was not the priesthood but the church. He has always believed that the only way to deepen understanding of the ordained ministry and to renew its life is to see it within the context of an authentic ecclesiology. The theology of the church that was still dominant in the 1930s was inadequate to the task. Narrowly juridical and highly apologetic, it focused almost exclusively on the hierarchy and on its distinctive powers and rights. To describe it Congar coined the phrase "hierarchology." The laity tended to be defined negatively as those who were not ordained and were considered generally as little more than objects of the concerns and activities of the clergy.

The Need for Renewal

The renewal of ecclesiology that took place immediately before and after the Second World War was provoked by a double concern, one properly theological and the other pastoral. The initial theological task was to overcome the abstract and ahistorical approach of neo-scholasticism. The call in France was for *ressourcement,* a return to the historical and biblical sources of faith. People sought an escape from the narrowness of the modern Catholic tradition by appealing to an older and richer one. Dominicans like Congar and Chenu turned to Aquinas and to other great scholastic figures whom they interpreted in an historical way. Jesuits like de Lubac helped to revive an interest in the patristic period. For Congar *ressourcement* came to embrace Protestant and Orthodox writers as well as classics of the Catholic tradition such as J.A. Moehler. As the period progressed and especially after Vatican II the appeal to the scriptures became more central, as did a willingness to read them with the tools of modern critical scholarship.

Parallel to this scholarly renewal and in part fed by it was a blossoming of pastoral activity. France and Belgium saw the rise of Catholic Action. In a variety of specialized forms it provided lay people an opportunity to become involved in an organized and official way in the mission and ministry of the church. Although the particular forms of Catholic Action lost their appeal in the post-conciliar period, it remains that they were key elements in the renewal that led to the "rediscovery" of the laity at Vatican II. The age of Catholic Action was also the age of the setting up and flowering of the *Mission de France*. A growing awareness of the depth of alienation of people from the church, especially among the working class, led to concerted efforts on the part of some priests to break out of traditional methods and structures and to develop new forms of evangelization and of witness. The most famous of these was the worker priest movement.

Although less involved in the details of pastoral developments than his mentor Chenu, Congar was profoundly influenced by them both in his general theology of the church and in his efforts to rethink the nature of the priesthood. One of his first major contributions to a renewed ecclesiology was *Lay People in the Church*, published in 1953 but largely based on lectures given in 1946 and 1948.[2] The project was novel. He wanted to define the situation of the laity not negatively but positively. A large book, it offers a compendium of the best of what was available at the time on the topic. Central to the presentation is the use of the threefold office of Christ. The laity, through faith and baptism, share in Christ's office as priest, prophet and king. The longest section is dedicated to the theme of priesthood.

The Meaning of Priesthood

Priesthood remained throughout most of Congar's career a fundamental category for dealing with both the laity and the ordained ministry. This is partly due to the affirmations and negations of both the reformation and its opponents. Luther's insistence on the priesthood of the faithful and Tridentine Catholicism's disregard of it made it an obvious focus for an attempt to develop in an ecumenical context a positive theology of the laity. The centrality of the category of priesthood at Trent and in the French school of spirituality made its use in regard to the ordained ministry self-evident. Congar affirms the priesthood of all believers, and as he does he begins the process of redefining the ministerial priesthood in relation to it.

Although other authors at the time related priesthood to the broader category of mediation or to the more spiritually oriented one of consecration, Congar consistently defined priesthood in terms of sacrifice. For him the two are inseparable. Thus, if all believers are in some sense priests, if together they form a royal priesthood, then they are called and enabled to offer some form of sacrifice. Congar calls it the sacrifice of life. A key text here is Romans 12:1. Although he uses the word "spiritual" of both the priesthood of the faithful and their sacrifice, he is not suggesting that they are unreal, for the spiritual is precisely what is most real. Both realities, moreover, are spiritual in a double sense. In the first place they bring to fulfillment the "spiritualizing" tendencies of prophets and psalmists who applied the language of cult to moral and religious attitudes and practices. Even more importantly, they are spiritual because they are rooted in the reality of Christ and in the gift of his Spirit. In Christ the very nature of priesthood and sacrifice is radically transformed.

The sacrifice that God ultimately asks of human beings is the sacrifice of themselves. This is the sense of the sacrifice of Jesus and this is what in him and through his Spirit becomes possible for believers. Congar appeals to the age old distinction between *res* and *sacramentum,* between the reality that the Christian dispensation serves and communicates and the external signs and symbols that mediate it. The *res* of Christianity is human life given over to God in worship and discipleship. Far from being metaphorical, the priesthood and the sacrifice of the faithful are what Christ's life and saving work are meant to foster.

The ordained ministry represents a distinctive participation in the threefold office of Christ, including naturally his priesthood. It is a function or service that is meant to build up the priesthood of the faithful. An absolutely key text to which Congar appeals repeatedly is Romans 15:16. It both provides a way of dealing with the fact that the NT nowhere calls leaders of the community "priests" and suggests how, from a NT perspective, "priesthood" relates to preaching. In Romans Paul speaks of his evangelical activity in relation to the life offering of the Gentiles as a priestly or sacral service. In the light of this, Congar argues that everything that a priest does that contributes to deepening the faith and Christian life of believers, everything, that is, that helps them to lead the kind of life that constitutes their spiritual sacrifice, is by that fact a priestly act.

In the pre-conciliar period Congar spoke on a number of occasions not of two but of three participations in the priesthood of Christ. The distinction between the first two of these is somewhat artificial. He calls the first the priesthood of a holy and dedicated life, the priesthood that in some sense can be identified with the Christian life as such. He relates it to the biblical phrase "royal priesthood" and to what Trent calls an "interior priesthood." Its liturgy is the liturgy of a life lived in imitation of Jesus and under the impulse of his Spirit.

The other two forms of priesthood are both related to the sacraments and to the external and public liturgy of the church. Here he distinguishes between a baptismal priesthood and a hierarchical or ministerial priesthood. His inspiration here is Aquinas' understanding of the sacramental character as involving some form of participation in acts of cult and worship. It is because of the baptismal character that believers are able to participate in the sacraments and especially in the eucharist in which in a real sense they are "legitimate concelebrants."

Instruments of Christ

As much as Congar insisted in the 1950s on the spiritual reality of the priesthood of all believers, he rejected any interpretation that would see the ordained as nothing more than organs of the priestly community. They are that in certain respects, but when it comes to the sacraments and especially to the eucharist, "it is the cult of the Lord that the priest above all celebrates; he is primarily the minister and representative of Jesus Christ; he celebrates *in persona Christi.*"[3]

Congar continued to refer to a threefold distinction in the priesthood right up to Vatican II. The council itself, however, decided to include his first two forms in its understanding of the priesthood of the faithful. By faith and baptism Christians are made to share in the priesthood of Christ and by that fact are enabled both to offer the sacrifice of life and to take an active part in the church's liturgy. The question here is more one of formulation than of anything else. Central for Congar at all stages of his life is a conviction about the radical transformation the NT represents in regard to the meaning of cult.

There is a tissue of texts including Romans 15:16, Philippians 2:7, Romans 12:1, 1 Peter 2:4–10 and Augustine's *City of God* X, 5, 6 to which Congar regularly refers when discussing the distinctively Christian understanding of cult. The same texts appear in PO 2. That extremely compact paragraph in which the call of some of the bishops at the council for priestly language was heeded contains a strong affirmation of the centrality of preaching and teaching to the priestly office. This way of understanding and relating the NT meaning of cult, the priesthood and sacrifice of the faithful, and the priesthood of the ordained is not abandoned by Congar in the post-conciliar period. For him they represent profound theological insights that take us to the heart of the Christian dispensation. They remain, however, in his mind surprisingly underdeveloped in contemporary theology.

In 1951 Congar published a thesis of the late Abbé Long-Hasselmans on the Catholic priesthood, including with it a number of critical remarks of his own.[4] He clearly thought it of considerable importance and in subsequent years referred back to it on several occasions. By the 1970s he was admitting that he would now have to formulate his criticisms somewhat differently, Hasselmans briefly evokes the use of priestly language in the NT and the early church and then offers the outline of a theological synthesis. The emphasis is on the priesthood of Christ and the priesthood of the faithful. Christ is the unique priest in whose priesthood all believers share. Through faith and baptism they constitute a priestly people, empowered to offer spiritual sacrifices, pleasing to God. Hasselmans does not see the ordained ministry as representing a distinctive participation in the priesthood of Christ. In terms of priesthood there is only, apart from that of Christ, the priesthood of the faithful. Presbyters are delegated by the community and established in their office to be of service to the whole. They are organs of the community helping to organize and direct its public life. Their basic power is one of jurisdiction.

The fundamental criticism of Congar is that Hasselmans fails to do justice to the sacramental nature of ordination and to the fact that the ordained participate in the priesthood of Christ in a distinctive way. Ordination and baptism represent two different ways of relating to Christ. Ordination is not simply an act of the community, even as inspired and guided by the Spirit. It is an act of the risen Christ mediated through the already existing office which itself is in historical continuity with the apostolic community.

While recognizing that in a certain sense the ordained are organs of the church, Congar insists that in other respects they are instruments of Christ. They were instituted by Christ before the church and are used by him to build it up. The relation of Christ to the church is both immanent and transcendent. The life of Christ is in the community of faith making it truly his body, and yet at the same time he is its head. He remains superior to it and continues to call, challenge, and nourish it until its final perfecting in the eschaton. It is this sense of the superiority of Christ to the church, this element of his being over against it, that is sacramentally expressed in the ordained ministry.

Congar appeals here to a favorite distinction of his in the preconciliar period, that between structure and life. Structure stands for what God in Christ has given to the church: the deposit of faith, the sacraments, and the apostolic ministry. They constitute the essence of the church, that without which it would cease to be. These gifts, however, are meant to bear fruit, to call forth a life, to become embodied in a believing community. He speaks in this regard of a hierarchical pole and a community pole. The community pole is on the side of life and represents the laity. It pertains not to the *esse,* the being of the church, but to its *bene esse,* its well-being.

It was with the language of structure and life that Congar tried to move beyond the then dominant ecclesiology that had no positive place for the laity. As helpful in some respects as the effort was, he later recognized its inadequacies. It remained too clerical, the hierarchy and the laity were too rigidly divided, and the latter failed to receive their full due. What was needed was a new starting place. This was to be provided by the council and its theology of the people of God.

Emphasizing the Community

Congar makes a great deal of the insertion of the second chapter of *LG* on the people of God before the chapter on the hierarchy. For him this was a clear affirmation that the primary reality in the church is not the hierarchy but the community, the whole assembly of believers, within which the ordained ministry is called to offer a service and fulfill a function. The step forward from *Lay People* was the recognition that the ministry is not above or outside the church but within it. At the time of the council, Congar believed that it would take more than one generation for theologians and church people to appreciate the implications of this emphasis and to develop adequate structures to embody it. History has already proved him right.

Closely aligned to the stress on the community was the rediscovery by Vatican II of the importance of charisms and of ministries in the plural. This of course was inspired by a rereading of the NT and especially of Paul. The implications of this for the ordained ministry are considerable. In these and other developments at and since Vatican II Congar sees a movement away from a view that had dominated the last thousand years of church history. His own development in some sense represents a progressive reappropriation of earlier understandings and practices that since the high middle ages had tended to be forgotten. The really delicate challenge in this process is to know what to do with the medieval developments. Are they simply to be rejected or can they in a reappropriation of earlier traditions be maintained even if inevitably understood now in a somewhat different way? Congar, unlike some others, has opted for the second position. It has left him exposed to criticism by both sides in a number of contemporary debates.

The great turning point in the history of the ordained ministry comes in the twelfth century. The earlier relation of the ministry to the community fades and is progressively replaced, at least theoretically, by its relation to the eucharist. The practice of "absolute" ordinations, i.e. ordinations without a reference to a particular ministry and community, heightens the tendency to think of the priest in terms of sacramental powers. It is at this period too that the language of sacramental character becomes common. Initially it is related to the fact that ordination is never repeated. In the thirteenth century, however, the character is interpreted in onto-logical terms and is associated with the power to "confect" the eucharist. It is this constellation of priest, character, and power over the eucharist that will dominate Trent and subsequent devel-opments. In the light of the NT and the early church, the medieval emphases represent at the very least a novelty and, in terms of balance, a distortion.

Vatican II, in Congar's judgment, marked a new stage, a step forward in the task of redressing the balance. Post-conciliar devel-opments rapidly went beyond the texts of the council, however, in the radicalism with which in the light of historical research and contemporary problems they questioned the validity of the medi-eval synthesis. Congar himself came to judge his own earlier contri-butions as too influenced by medieval distinctions and presupposi-tions. He found himself much more attracted to NT emphases, but even as he did he tried to maintain what he believed to be a distinctively Catholic understanding.[5]

Icons of Christ

As much as he insists that the ordained ministry has to be seen within the community and in relation to other charisms and minis-tries, Congar refuses to view it exclusively in terms of the commu-nity. The need is to find a balance between "from below" and "from above," between the church and the risen Christ, between the apostolicity of the whole community and that of the ordained ministry. As much as the ordained ministry represents and issues from the church, it continues to be called into being by the risen Christ. Ordination remains a sacrament and not simply a way by which the community delegates certain of its members to fulfill an office. As a sacrament it involves a present and real intervention of Christ through the Spirit effecting a change within the ordained so that they can act *in persona Christi,* so that they can be icons of Christ. Although the activity of Christ in the ministers reaches a particular intensity in the sacraments and especially in the eucha-rist, it is a factor in preaching and pastoral responsibilities as well.

Congar has always understood ordination in relation to office or ministry within the community. The ordained have a function to fulfill. This stress on the functional aspect of ministry is not a denial of the ontological. The very nature of the Christian community with its special relation to Christ and the Spirit means that the functional quality of its ministry is rooted in ontology, an ontology, however, different from the more fundamental and significant ontology of charity bestowed by baptism. For a long time Congar had difficulty with Pius XII's affirmation that the priesthood of the ordained differed in essence and not just in degree from that of the faithful. At the council he attempted to offer alternative formulations but without success. When the phrase was inserted into LG 10, Congar argued that it could be interpreted in a positive way. Ministers are not super Christians. By ordination they share in the priesthood of Christ in a different, i.e. in a ministerial way.

Traditionally and again at Vatican II the distinctive nature of the priesthood of the ordained has been tied up with the notion of sacramental character. This has come under attack from a variety of points of view in the post-conciliar period. Historical research has shown that it only became significant in the middle ages and that even then there was no single understanding of it. There has even been on the popular level a tendency to simplify it until it took on an almost "magical" quality. The ontological language sometimes associated with it has been seen as justifying a one-sided emphasis on priesthood as a state of life and as reinforcing a tendency to separate the priest as a sacred or cultic figure from the life of the community. Congar argues against the basic thrust of these approaches and insists that the theology of character that has been developed is in no sense definitive. The central issue historically had to do with the non-repeatable nature of the sacrament. The eastern tradition holds this but expresses it in a different way. It refers to the grace and charism of God that is never rescinded.

Ministry not Power

For Congar, the emphasis on the connection between character and power is both ambivalent and unnecessary. It developed at a time when the priest was understood in relation not to the community but to the eucharist and to Christ in whose name and person he was empowered to offer it. Congar has always felt hesitation about the use of the language of "power" in this regard. He prefers Augustine's insight that in matters of grace and the sacraments the power belongs to the risen Christ. What the church and the priest exercise is a *ministerium*. A sensitivity to this has been kept alive in the eastern tradition by its emphasis on the role in the sacraments of the epiclesis or prayer to the Spirit. This reference to Augustine and the east underlines that Congar's talk of the functional nature of ministry was never intended to be simply sociological. It is rooted in a profoundly religious understanding of office. One is a minister of Christ, the Christ who gave himself for us in his earthly life and who continues through his Spirit to nourish and guide his church.

Related to the idea of character is the notion of an eternal priesthood, *sacerdos in aeternum*. For Congar this can only be applied to Christ. Following Aquinas he argues that the sacramental character as related to cult is restricted "to the liturgy of the present church." The structural dimension of the church is conditioned by its existence in "the in-between times." Once the church is brought to its fulfillment, and God is indeed all in all, forms of external mediation will have no significance.

If the theology and language of character are dispensable, ordination remains a sacramental act in which something of genuine significance takes place. By the imposition of hands the ordained become members of the college or *ordo* of ministers and are related to the ministry of the apostles. They are enabled to represent Christ who is both immanent in and transcendent to the community of faith. Acting in the name of Christ, priest, prophet and king, they exercise Christ's messianic ministry within and in certain cases over against the church.

For Congar ordination is the ordinary way by which one assumes leadership of a community and is enabled to preside at its eucharist. In the pre-Vatican II period he rejected the possibility of any other approach. Since the council his position has become more nuanced. In a 1969 review of Küng's *The Church*, for example, he admitted the possibility of a community providing itself with an ordained minister in case of grave necessity.[6] To justify this he appealed to the notion of "economy," the idea that God is not bound by the structures and institutions that he has established but can and does go beyond them for the good of the church and the continuance of Christ's saving work in all its fullness. On different occasions Congar has expressed his conviction that a theory of economy is essential if Catholicism is to deal with all the anomalies that history reveals in regard to orders and to apostolic succession. This approach separates him from those who would argue to the same practice but on the grounds of the universal priesthood of the baptized or in terms of an exclusively pneumatological and charismatic understanding of ministry. For Congar the present intervention of the Spirit has to be coupled with an historical connection through apostolic succession with the Incarnate Word.

Balance and Wholeness

One of the more striking features of Congar's theological efforts has been his concern for synthesis and integration. He has tried to bring together what, in his judgment, the post-medieval and post-reformation church tended to divide: pope and bishops, priests and laity, liturgy and life. The same is true of christology and pneumatology, the understanding of the respective roles in the Christian dispensation of Christ and the Spirit. Western Christianity in the medieval period embraced a kind of Christomonism. It rarely referred to the presence or activity of the Holy Spirit. Christ, as both the historical Jesus and the risen Christ, dominated theology and piety. It was Christ who instituted the sacraments and who set up the apostolic ministry. It is in the name and person of the risen Christ that priests preside at the eucharist. Wherever this one-sided emphasis on Christ combined with a juridical mentality, an institutional view of the church flourished.

Almost from the beginning of his career Congar was concerned to bring back to ecclesiology a sense of the Spirit and of its essential role in fostering the life of the community. Because the Spirit is poured out on the whole church, a pneumatic ecclesiology inevitably sees the ministry in close relationship to the activity of all believers. A sense of the presence of the Spirit also deepens one's religious understanding of ordination. The ritual offers much more than historical continuity with the apostles. It is a new and present act of the risen Christ through his Spirit building up the church here and now.

Congar's publication of J.A. Moehler's 1827 *The Unity of the Church* in French translation in 1938 was a signal of his commitment to the development of a Spirit-oriented ecclesiology. His concern for pneumatology culminated in the three-volume *I Believe in the Holy Spirit* of the 1970s. The work is also an eloquent testimony to his great love and knowledge of eastern Orthodoxy. For all the emphasis on the Spirit, however, Congar here as elsewhere sought a balance. Christology and pneumatology are finally inseparable; they mutually define and reinforce one another. This conviction has implications for ecclesiology and for the understanding of ministry.

The episcopate and the presbyterate are inseparable from the apostolic ministry and its succession. While rejecting the "pipeline" theory of succession, Congar insists on the importance of historical continuity. The doctrine of the incarnation demands that space and time, history and tradition be taken seriously. In the Catholic tradition this principle has been understood to be embodied in a special way in the fact of apostolic succession. In this as in other areas Congar has changed his position over the years, not so much by denying what he first affirmed but by understanding it in the light of new insights as these came to him.

Ecumenical activities, the experience of the council, and historical research convinced Congar that his initial understanding of apostolic succession had to be broadened in two ways. He came to realize in the first place that apostolic succession was understood initially as a safeguard for apostolic doctrine and that therefore the apostolicity of the church depends more on the apostolic nature of its faith than on the mere fact of historical continuity in the ministry. Apostolicity, moreover, applies to the whole church and not just to its leaders. All believers are to ensure that the church continues to embody the faith and life of the apostles and to carry on their mission and ministry. As with the phenomenon of priesthood, the recognition of the apostolicity of the community does not undermine or render irrelevant a particular embodiment of the apostolic ministry within it. Once again we have a ministry, a service, that is meant to foster and build up the apostolicity of the community as a whole. To do this it has a genuine authority analogous to that of the apostles.

The Language of Priesthood

More than many Catholic theologians, Congar continued after the council to use priestly language for the ordained ministry. It was not as if he were unaware of its ambiguity. Although its introduction in the third century is not simply to be dismissed as an unfortunate error, it did in fact introduce a shift in understanding that over the centuries became one-sided. Contemporary developments are clearly seeking a better balance. The ministry can still be described as priestly, however, because it serves both Christ the priest and the priestly community. As functional or ministerial as the priesthood of the ordained is, it involves an original participation in the priesthood of Christ, one which grounds their public ministry within the church.

For Congar, Christian priesthood, whether that of Christ, the baptized, or the ordained, always implies prophetic and pastoral dimensions. If, for a long time, he continued to use sacerdotal language, it was because he understood the gospel priesthood as essentially evangelical and apostolic. With Vatican II he recognizes the episcopacy as the fundamental ministry in the light of which all ministry has to be understood. This, by itself, underlines its pastoral nature.

In the preface to a 1978 book on the history of the phrases *in persona Christi* and *in persona ecclesiae,* Congar summed up the shift that had been taking place over the previous decades in Catholic theology of the ministry, a shift to which he himself had contributed in no small degree.[7] He began with a question: Is a priest/presbyter the qualified celebrant of the eucharist because he is the ordained leader of the community or is he its leader because he has received through ordination the power to consecrate the eucharistic gifts?

The traditional answer from Aquinas to Vatican II was the latter. This position emphasized the relation of the priest to Christ. He acts, especially in the eucharist, *in persona Christi.* The tendency today is to approach the issue from the perspective of the church. Among the many gifts and ministries that Christ through the Spirit calls forth in the community is one which has a special responsibility for word and sacrament and which is also called to coordinate and draw forth the other ministries. This double task is at the heart of what is called presiding in a community. It is because they accept this broader responsibility that priests preside at the eucharist. Although the whole community participates actively in the celebration, the ordained minister alone consecrates the gifts and in doing so acts as the icon, the representative of Christ. Fulfilling Christ's role in the celebration, priests act *in persona Christi.*

For Congar this more ecclesiological and ministerial approach is firmly rooted in the tradition of the early church. The dominant model is the pastoral one. To the degree that *vice Christi* (in the place of Christ) can be applied here at all, it is related not primarily to the power to consecrate, but to the responsibility to build up and preside over the church. As Congar puts it with typical understatement, this approach is different from the one that dominated much of Catholic theology since the triumph of scholasticism.

4
K. Rahner: Office as Service of the Word

That Karl Rahner's contribution to the renewal of Catholic systematic theology in the twentieth century has been considerable is widely recognized. That he wrote as much as he did on ecclesiology and on the ordained ministry is perhaps less well known. His status and influence as well as his obvious differences in approach and methodology from Congar make him a significant and complementary witness to efforts both before and after Vatican II to rethink the Catholic understanding of the ministerial priesthood.[1]

As with Congar, Rahner's opinions in this area underwent considerable development. In the 1940s and 1950s he was much concerned with breaking out of the narrowness of neo-scholasticism. If Congar did this primarily by appealing to the historical Aquinas and to the broader tradition of the church, Rahner tried to open neo-scholasticism from within. He asked questions, drew implications and brought together into new relationships affirmations that previously had existed only in separate tracts.

Rahner was very much interested in the contemporary church and in the pastoral challenges facing it. By the beginning of Vatican II he had already committed himself with others to producing a multi-volume handbook of pastoral theology. In it he argued the necessity of relating theory and practice more closely, especially in regard to ecclesiology and to concrete decisions about how the church is to fulfill its mission in the contemporary world.

Openness to the actual situation of the church was a major factor in the development of Rahner's theology of the ministry in the post-conciliar period. The shortage of priests, the renewal of the diaconate, the presence of full-time lay ministers or pastoral assistants as they are called in Germany, the growing secularization of western European culture: these and other phenomena seemed to demand a fairly radical rethinking of both the theology and the practice of ministry. What facilitated this rethinking was the more nuanced picture of the origins and early developments of church office as this was emerging from recent biblical and historical scholarship.

A third factor that should at least be mentioned is the ecumenical movement. Without being an ecumenist in the narrow sense, Rahner was fully aware of, and made important contributions to, the dialogue, especially as it was taking place in Germany. He raised questions about issues in the theology of ministry that the traditional manuals took for granted but which, he insisted, were still open to debate.

Given the few pages that are available to deal with Rahner's theology, there will be no attempt here to trace in detail the changes that it underwent. References will be made to these, but the overall treatment will not be chronological. For all the development in his thought, Rahner remained remarkably consistent in regard to some key convictions. More systematic and less historical than Congar, he arrived relatively early at certain insights which he subsequently mined in ever more fruitful ways.

Ministry as Office

The key category for Rahner in thinking about the ordained ministry is *Amt* or office. German language areas have not experienced any dramatic shift in terminology analogous to what has happened in English in regard to "ministry." Although this latter word is now used by Catholics for a wide range of full- and part-time activities, it was earlier mainly a Protestant term largely restricted to official or ordained ministry. *Amt* remains for many in German the term for official or ordained ministry, with the more generic *Dienst* or service corresponding to some extent to our broad sense of "ministry."

Amt as Rahner uses it has institutional or structural overtones. It is what develops almost inevitably in any community or group that is of a certain size and that wants to survive for any length of time. Organization and structure are for the community and not vice versa. *Amt* should be seen as a *Dienst,* a service to the community within which and for which it exists. What makes ecclesial office distinctive is the nature of the church. To spell that out one has to keep in mind all the central elements of Rahner's theology: the reality of God as both the creator and goal of all that is; the fact of God's universal offer of self-communication in what is called grace; the irreversible and triumphant historical offer and acceptance of that grace in the person and destiny of Jesus; the continuation of his offer of salvation in the community of believers called the church.

Rahner's ecclesiology is in certain respects an ecclesiology from above; it insists on the already given in Christian eschatology and sees the visible church as a sacrament of universal salvation. He both relativizes the historical church and its means of grace by stressing the universality of God's offer of salvation, and gives it an irreplaceable significance by rooting it in the once and for all life of the Word made flesh.

Office exists within the church. Even if in dependence on the apostolic ministry, it is the church to a large degree that gives its structure to itself. It certainly has a great deal of authority over the forms that it takes and over the determination of how people should be designated for it. And yet office is not simply from below. Ministers receive a call and mandate from Christ. To some extent they act in his name. At the same time, however, and Rahner insists on this with increasing emphasis, they do not exist apart from the community as some kind of spiritual elite. They are called in the midst of the community to exercise an authority that in the last analysis belongs to it.

The Unity of Ecclesial Office

Rahner stresses the unity of office. If the church itself is to be an ordered and unified community, then office must serve both unity and order. Although he refers occasionally to the threefold office of Christ and to its application at Vatican II to church office, he largely disregards it in developing his own position. The same is true of the traditional distinction between the power of orders and the power of jurisdiction. The distinction is unclear and ultimately inadequate. Behind the distinctions is a more profound unity. Existing in order to provide a service within the church, office is conferred by ordination which communicates the powers required to exercise it and the personal grace without which its exercise will be largely fruitless.

If office is basically one, it can and indeed must be divided into various levels. This is clearly what happened in the development of the threefold distinction between the episcopacy, the presbyterate, and the diaconate. In his earlier writings Rahner assumed that even if these three forms of office did not go back to Jesus, they could still be seen as existing by divine right because they developed in the period of the primitive church. In the 1970s he became less certain that this was in fact the case. By this time he accepted the papacy and the episcopacy as of divine right and believed that the presbyterate probably was too, but he no longer claimed that it was certain. The fact of the matter is that there is no witness for the threefold office until the second decade of the second century and that even then the structure was far from universal.

The notion that office is fundamentally one and that its powers and responsibilities can be distributed to various people and in various combinations is a basic conviction of Rahner. As the years go by his sense of flexibility here increases although the principle remains the same. He argues, for example, that there could be more sacramental participations in the one office than the three we presently recognize. In this regard he is sympathetic to medieval theologians who affirmed the sacramental nature of the minor orders. At the same time he recognizes no dogmatic basis for insisting that the episcopal office be exercised by a single person. The collegial principle is so much a part of office even at the highest level that there is no reason why it could not be operative at the local level as well. A group could exercise episcopal authority over a diocese.

This sensitivity to the collegial nature of office influenced Rahner's approach to the presbyterate, particularly in the years around Vatican II. Priests are first of all members of a presbyterium with and under a local bishop. They are this before being appointed to a local community. The parallel here is with the pope and bishops. Later Rahner became critical of Vatican II's description of presbyters as helpers of the bishop. Such a formulation, he thought, undermines the relative independence and genuinely collegial responsibility of the priest and is a reflection of an "episcopal ideology."

From the beginning to the end of his career, Rahner repeatedly pointed out the lack of clarity in the theological distinction between bishops and presbyters. The only thing ultimately that bishops alone seem able to do is to ordain other bishops. Contemporary pastors seem to correspond to bishops in the early church while present bishops are more like metropolitans or other early supra-diocesan authorities. The confusing lack of clarity and the fluid boundaries between the different orders reinforces Rahner's conviction that ecclesial office is finally one and that the church has more flexibility in distributing its various powers and responsibilities than ordinarily thought. This applies not only to the sacramental area—presbyters as ordinary ministers of confirmation and possible extraordinary ministers of presbyteral ordination—but also to the jurisdictional. Bishops could easily bind themselves by law to act in a strictly collegial manner within their dioceses.

In the 1970s Rahner seemed to move away to some extent from the collegial starting point for his theology of the presbyterate. Practical developments convinced him that the future of the church lay with grass roots communities, with small local groups of believers that develop around different interests and which from within themselves call forth their own leaders. These, of course, would have to be recognized by the large church and ordained by a bishop, but they come to the fore as the natural leaders of an already existing community. The shift from the universal church to the local community has other implications, including the recognition of the right of the local church to the eucharist and therefore to a priest. The phenomenon of full-time lay pastoral assistants in parishes without priests is for Rahner an anomaly. It only exists because of the law of celibacy and the regulation about the non-ordination of women. People who exercise leadership in an official way within a stable church community should be or-dained whatever their sex or marital status. The separation of leadership of the community from presiding at the eucharist is a mistake that will eventually undermine Catholic ecclesiology. The leader of the eucharist must be the pastoral leader of the commu-nity and vice versa.

As much as Rahner poses questions to the traditional theology of office and as much as he insists on the flexibility that the church has in its regard, he sees the ordained ministry as belonging to the essence of the church. It is clearly willed by Christ, and endowed with gifts of the Spirit. These relate primarily to pastoral leader-ship, to authoritative teaching of the word, and to the celebration of the sacraments, especially of the eucharist.

Office and Charism

Office, for all its importance, cannot be seen in isolation. It is not the only active agent of the church's self-realization. Where Congar and others would make this point by insisting on the priest-hood of the faithful, Rahner focuses on the phenomenon of charism, a theme that he emphasized even before the council. It flows in part from his high doctrine of grace and his understanding of it in terms of the Spirit. For Rahner, as for Aquinas before him, the institutional elements in Christianity, including word, sacra-ment and office, exist for the spiritual reality of God's self-communication. That is the *res,* the reality that the institution as sign or *sacramentum* is meant to foster. This traditional sense was reinforced by his reading of Ignatius of Loyola. What he learned from the founder of the Jesuits was the possibility of the experience of God in everyday life. God's grace and gifts exist outside of the confines of the hierarchical and the sacramental. Vatican II's redis-covery of the NT teaching on charisms reinforced this emphasis.

The fact that he sees ministry in terms of *Amt,* office, makes it natural for Rahner, especially against the background of German Protestant theology, to formulate the relation between the or-dained and the non-ordained in terms of charism and office, charism and institution. If Vatican II opened Catholics to the fact that there are charisms as well as office in the church, more radical questioning in the 1970s led Rahner to wonder whether charism should not be seen as *the* essential reality which office finally is meant to foster and serve. That the existence of both charism and office in the church will lead to tension and conflict is for Rahner self-evident. Although ordinarily office, in the name of unity and good order, will make the final judgment about charisms, there is no guarantee that this will always work out or in fact be the right solution. Successful collaboration between charism and institution will be itself a gift of the Spirit.

Declericalization

Even in the pre-conciliar period Rahner was deeply concerned about what he perceived to be an unhealthy separation of the clergy from the laity. In homilies at first masses he stressed the humanity of the priest. Although called to fulfill a special function in the church he is and remains a human being, a brother of all the faithful. Whether because of Rahner or not, this concern was brought to Vatican II by the German bishops. In the post-conciliar period Rahner insists even more on the fact that the priest is not someone set apart, someone who lives in a special religious sphere over against the so-called profane world of the laity. He shares their situation but he does it in order precisely to bring them the saving, healing, elevating word of the gospel.

In *The Shape of the Church to Come,* his contribution to the debates surrounding the 1974 German Synod, Rahner called for the declericalization of the church.[2] This was not an attack on the ordained ministry as such, but rather on certain ways in which it was both understood and exercised. The world is changing and so is the place of the church in it. With the increasing secularization of western culture the church is gradually being transformed from a "Volkskirche," a church to which people naturally belong because they are born in particular nations or regions, to a voluntary church in which people are members because they have come to a personal act of faith. The authority of the office-holder in such a church will depend not so much on the fact of office as on the free response of the community and therefore to a great extent on the office-holder's own spiritual gifts and personal authority.

In a declericalized church, office-holders will see themselves as servants of the community. They will also recognize and listen to the stirring of the Spirit among the faithful. Knowing their own limits, they will foster and nurture the contribution of everyone to the common good. The humility of such office-holders will be reinforced by their conviction that in the church there is a hierarchy of grace as well as a hierarchy of office and that the latter exists to serve the former. On several occasions Rahner had recourse to a rather bold analogy to make his point. A chess club exists so that good chess will be played. The officers of the club, the ones who accept responsibility to see that physical and other requirements are met so that the club can flourish, are not the reason for the existence of the club. They exist and fulfill their responsibilities so that the club's true goal can be achieved.

Preaching and Teaching

Responsibility for the word and for preaching and teaching in their many forms is central to Rahner's understanding of ecclesial office. His first substantial article on the priesthood, published in 1942, argued that a one-sidedly cultic or sacramental view of the Christian ministry was inadequate.[3] In it, as in Christ's own ministry, the priestly and prophetic vocations are combined. The Christian priesthood is essentially prophetic and apostolic. At this stage he argues from the sacrament to the word and not, as later, in the reverse order. Sacraments, as means of bringing to bear the saving work of Christ on individuals, appeal to and presuppose faith. The word is of the essence of the sacrament, for it both determines the natural symbol in its specifically Christian signification and appeals to those participating in the sacrament to open themselves to it in faith. The word which is part of the sacrament calls for the further word of preaching. This both prepares and unpacks the meaning of the sacrament. The ministerial priesthood is thus both cultic and prophetic and that in the most profound of unities. The prophetic grows out of the cultic and facilitates its final realization within a whole life of faith, hope and love.

This article is one of the few in which the category of "priesthood" plays a central role. Like Congar in the pre-Vatican II period Rahner is anxious to eliminate possible misunderstandings. Priestly language within the Christian dispensation is relativized in three directions. Most profoundly it is a ministerial priesthood totally dependent upon, and at the service of, the priesthood of Christ. The priesthood of Christ, moreover, is shared in by all the faithful and not just the ordained. In fact the general priesthood precedes the ministerial priesthood and is not to be seen as simply a weakened extension of it. Christian priesthood, finally, as already indicated, is never merely cultic. It has a necessary apostolic and prophetic thrust to it.

In a striking and imaginative 1956 article entitled "Priest and Poet," the emphasis on the word has become even more marked.[4] The priest, like the poet, is a person of the word. If the poet's vocation is to keep alive, proclaim, and make resonant the *Urworte,* the great but simple words that remind us of the depths of our humanity, the priest is called to be the messenger and proclaimer of the word of God. His word, Rahner insists, is an active word, an effective word. The priest is less a theologian than a preacher, the herald of the event of grace and salvation.

Grace for Rahner is present to all of human life. It is often pre-verbal and pre-conscious. It has, however, an inner dynamism toward articulation. It is only in the word that our graced transcendence can become known, that the graced person can become present to self in a fully human way. The word of God that the priest proclaims exists at various levels of intensity. Its most concentrated form is to be found in the sacraments and above all in the eucharist. By a brilliant reversal, the Tridentine emphasis on the power of the priest to offer the eucharist becomes in Rahner's view the highest form of the responsibility to proclaim the word.

In various articles in subsequent years Rahner deepens his theology of the word and applies it ever more systematically to the sacraments.[5] The word of preaching itself is understood as an "exhibitive" word, a word in which the reality about which one speaks is present in what is said. Because this is the saving reality of Jesus Christ, its presence gives the word of preaching an effective power for salvation. What is true of all authentic Christian preaching is also true of the sacraments. Here the analogous character of the word becomes evident. Sacraments represent the highest realization of the fundamental nature of the word of God as mediating and effectively rendering present the deed of salvation. In the sacraments the church which is both the hearer and the bearer of the word achieves a particularly intense form of self-realization. The sacrament can be subsumed under the general concept of the effective word of God.

In a 1966 article on ecclesial office Rahner argues that *ministerium verbi,* the ministry of the word, in the comprehensive sense outlined above, can be understood to be *the* function of the ordained ministry.[6] The same point is made in a brief but programmatic 1969 article. "The Point of Departure for Determining the Nature of the Priestly Office."[7] His rejection of sacramental power as the starting point is not a rejection of the teaching of Trent. It is simply a recognition that as a starting point it not only creates serious pastoral problems but also lacks a biblical basis. Without denying Trent's affirmations, he situates them within a different context. If the Tridentine starting point is inadequate, so, says Rahner, is the effort of Kasper, Ratzinger and others to begin with community leadership. The key is the word. "The priest is someone who is commissioned by the church as a whole and therefore officially to preach the word of God and that in relation to an at least potentially given community. The sacramentally highest forms of this word are entrusted to him."[8]

Even as Rahner insisted on the centrality of the word in his theology of office, he was perfectly aware that it was only one approach. He knew, for example, that in the NT the most obvious unifying concept for church office is that of community leadership. By the late 1970s he seems to have come around to this point of view himself. In a 1977 article he agreed with the general tendency in contemporary theology to think of the priest in analogy to the bishop in the local church.[9] Given the nature of the church, this leadership involves preaching and teaching and the gathering of the community for worship and the eucharist, but the unifying center of office is now pastoral leadership.

This emphasis on the pastoral aspect of office brings Rahner closer to the NT and to the position of Congar. As genuine as is his acceptance of this perspective, however, it in no sense undermines all that he had said previously about the centrality of the word. It is certainly the latter which from beginning to end directed Rahner's understanding and living out of his own vocation as a priest. This comes out most eloquently toward the end of his life in reflections on what it is to be a Jesuit today, reflections which he later described as his spiritual testament. The stress is on preaching and teaching and on mystagogy, the leading of people into an experience of the God of grace.[10]

Priestly Holiness

Like Congar, Rahner regularly speaks of the ordained ministry in functional terms. The concept itself of office suggests organizational and other tasks within a community. To be ordained is to accept certain pastoral, teaching, and worship responsibilities. Reference has already been made to his use of the analogy of the chess club. If office, however, is functional, it is not *merely* functional; it has a profound religious significance, for the minister as well as for the community. The major point of his already cited 1942 article was that the priesthood has fundamental implications for priestly *Existenz,* for the being and life of the priest. Rahner argues in that article not from the priest's cultic functions, but from his prophetic ones. To preach the word effectively one has to live what one preaches. In spite of the strong anti-Donatist tradition in the Catholic understanding of the ministry, Rahner insists on the crucial importance of priestly holiness. As objectively valid as sacraments are, they demand a response in faith from those who participate in them. This has to be stirred and facilitated by preachers. To do this, however, they cannot be content with preaching objective truths unrelated to their own personalities and experience. In matters of faith and religion the objective must be brought alive by passing through the subjectivity of the preacher.

This insistence on the importance of the quality of faith, hope, and love of the ordained is, if anything, intensified in Rahner's post-conciliar writings. It is reinforced by the increasingly diaspora situation in which the church finds itself. In a more and more secular world in which faith itself is such a challenge, an essential requirement for church leaders is that they be people of faith, people for whom God is a living reality, someone whom they have themselves experienced in their own lives.

Much of Rahner's theology comes together around the ordained ministry and the way that it should be exercised today. His life and practice reinforce and help to interpret what he says theologically. In spite of the apparent absence of the divine in modern culture, God is present in it, but in a more hidden way than in the past. Grace as the self-communication of God remains the inner entelechy of human history and of the life of individuals. In Christ this hidden presence has become historically and definitively visible. The church exists to bear witness to this presence of grace, to offer thanks for it, to celebrate it in word and sacrament, and to help its own members to live it both more profoundly and more consciously.

Priests are not holy persons who come from God to a Godless world. They are not mediators in any traditional sense, but rather people who in the world and in the community of faith accept the responsibility of religious leadership, of giving explicit witness in all that they are and do to what God and Christ are effecting in the world. In this sense priests belong to God and are religious persons. The necessary prerequisite for this is that they have experienced God, that they are to some degree mystics, and that they can lead others into the same experience.

Rahner's functional language makes sense. One is ordained for something, to fulfill a religious and evangelical task. Because of the religious nature of the task, and because it is carried out within and in the name of the church which is itself the sacrament of salvation, it is not just an office. It is a reality of the Spirit. Priests are called by God and in the sacrament of ordination are endowed with the powers required to fulfill their office and the grace and gifts without which their ministry will be in vain. There is a spiritual ontology to ecclesial office. Even more important for the actual excercise of office is Rahner's insight that ontological affirmations without an insistence on a complementary life are of little value. In a way that is both traditionally Ignatian and surprisingly modern, Rahner has brought the person of the ordained minister into the very center of his theology of church office.

5
J. Ratzinger: A Christocentric Emphasis

Almost twenty-five years younger than Rahner and Congar, Joseph Ratzinger was just beginning his university teaching when John XXIII announced his intention to convene Vatican II. Unlike his two older colleagues his theological education was neither Thomistic nor neo-scholastic. After a doctoral thesis on Augustine's ecclesiology, he wrote his "habilitation" or second dissertation, qualifying him to teach at the university level, on Bonaventure's theology of history. The later work both deepened his appreciation for eschatology and reinforced his commitment to a christocentric approach to theology.

In a series of articles appearing immediately before the council, Ratzinger outlined key aspects of his understanding of both the church and its ministry. Although he still maintains much of what he then affirmed, on some points post-conciliar developments have led him to shift his emphasis. To suggest why and how this came about will be one of the concerns of the following pages.[1]

Because much of what he has written on ecclesiology and on church office has been in the form of talks or articles requested for specific occasions, his starting point and the relative weight he has given to different aspects of the issues in question have tended to vary. In a number of early articles, for example, he begins his reflection on the church with an analysis of the NT word *ecclesia*. Etymologically it suggests a coming together, a gathering of people in response to a call, in this case to the call of the gospel. If the church is the people of God, it is such precisely as called together by God's word. Once assembled, the church becomes the "tent," the place where the word of God dwells. Church and word are inseparable.

This kind of ecclesiology inevitably gives a priority to preaching and teaching. Such was clearly the focus of the apostolic ministry but it is also central to the ministry of bishops and presbyters. Office in the church exists primarily to serve the word of God. This first task, however, is inseparable from a second. The church called together by the gospel is to celebrate the eucharist and in doing so to render present in its midst the power for life of the death and resurrection of Jesus. Sharing in the eucharistic body, the community itself becomes the body of Christ. Over time Ratzinger came to attach more significance to what he calls a eucharistic ecclesiology. If on the one hand the eucharist builds up and nourishes the church, the church itself exists to celebrate the eucharist in all its many dimensions. Office is thus tied up with the sacraments as well as with the word. It entails in particular presiding at the community's eucharist. Because Christian liturgy has what Ratzinger calls a cosmic dimension, presiding at it has pastoral implications as wide as life itself.

Ministry as *Diakonia*

In 1959 Ratzinger published a little book on Christian "Brotherhood."[2] Although the ministry is not the central theme, it is touched on in ways that are quite significant. Like Congar in his early writings, Ratzinger insists on the radical unity and equality of all members of the church. He cites in this regard Galatians 3:28 and Matthew 23:8–11. The latter text, in particular, in which Jesus tells his followers to call no one rabbi or father or master because all are brothers and sisters, can and should be used, he says, against the exaggerated preoccupation in church history with titles and honors. He laments the fact that Cyprian and later bishops tended to restrict the language of "brothers" to the episcopate and by that fact to undermine the earlier Christian experience of a common "brotherhood" uniting all believers.

At this point Ratzinger suggests that what is distinctive of NT ministry is that it is a *diakonia* or service. It is in no sense to be identified with "priesthood" as it exists in the history of religions. If on a purely phenomenological level the Christian ministry has similarities with priesthoods of other religions, this reflects the ever inadequate nature of our response to the gospel and the fact that in the course of history the Christian ministry has undergone influences of a non-Christian nature. He indicates as significant the fact that the sixth sacrament is known in the language of the church as *ordo* and not as *sacerdotium*.

Other early articles also insist on the importance of *diakonia*. Office or ministry is a service in and to the church. If Catholicism adds office to the Lutheran emphasis on word and sacrament, it does not put it on the same level as the other two. They ground the unity of the church and are of themselves causes of it. Office exists to serve them and not to exercise domination over them. The language of *diakonia* also throws light on the relation of the or-dained to the community as a whole. They offer "a service to the general priesthood of the faithful, and within that context, a ser-vice of order, but also a service to the freedom of the Spirit."[3]

Another article[4] states that church authority does not stand over against the community but rather within it. The Spirit is pres-ent in the body of Christ and continues through its various mem-bers to offer witness to itself. The laity are not to be thought of as merely passive but rather as active bearers of the word. The fact that office is "within" the church, however, does not mean that bishops are simply representatives of the people. They represent Christ from whom they have received both their mission and their consecration. When they speak definitively about the gospel, they do not speak on behalf of the community but rather on behalf of, and as commissioned by, the risen Lord. This markedly christologi-cal emphasis will be a constant element in Ratzinger's theology of the ministry.

Vatican II

Ratzinger was actively involved in the work of Vatican II both as an official peritus and as a theologian consultant for Cardinal

Frings of Cologne. His published reports on its various sessions reflect an enthusiasm for much that it was able to achieve.[5] He saw it as marking the end of an anti-Modernist mentality and as beginning the process of a genuine renewal of the church from the scriptures. He welcomed its christocentric focus particularly in regard to ecclesiology. The stress on the church as body of Christ and as sacrament as well as the whole thrust of the liturgical renewal offered, he believed, the possibility of a renewed understanding of the ordained ministry, one that would be less juridical, but also less isolated from the community. The implied ecclesiology of the document on the liturgy promised to free the church from "the hierarchical narrowness" of the recent past and to return it to its sacramental roots. In the same way he applauded the effort to overcome the traditional distinction between orders and jurisdiction. The priest celebrating the eucharist is not performing a religious act apart from the community. He is presiding at a corporate act in which all actively participate. Liturgical and pastoral responsibilities are not to be divided; the one flows over into the other. The church itself is primarily a liturgical community at the center of whose life is the eucharist. Church office is thus focused on preaching and presiding; its pastoral role is inseparable from its service at the table of the Lord.

The emphasis on the eucharist is at the same time an emphasis on the local church. The universal church, while present in eucharistic communities, is itself built up as a communion of churches. The fundamental unity of the faith that is professed and the mystery that is celebrated demands an office of unity. This is provided at the local level by bishops and then at the universal level by the pope.

Ratzinger was extremely positive about the decree on the Ministry and Life of Presbyters (PO).[6] He believed that it marked a decisive step forward, not least of all from an ecumenical point of view. From the beginning of his theological career Ratzinger took seriously the challenges represented by the Protestant reformation and in particular those formulated by Luther. The German reformer had reacted in the name of the NT against the one-sided emphasis in the late medieval understanding of ministry on priesthood and sacrifice. In opposition to all such views, he proclaimed the primacy of the word. While judging Luther to have gone too far, Ratzinger admitted that patristic and even more medieval theologies of office had not done sufficient justice to what was most distinctive about the NT understanding of ministry. They had tended too rapidly to apply to the Christian ministry universal concepts of priesthood that by themselves were inadequate to the transformation in priestly categories represented by Christ. PO, Ratzinger felt, went a long way to meet Luther's concerns. It begins with the notion of the church as a community of faith and affirms that the first task of the ministry is the preaching of the word. This preaching comes to its high point in the eucharist in which the death and resurrection of Jesus is proclaimed.

Ratzinger was particularly enthusiastic about what in fact was a major contribution of Congar to the document, the attempt to rediscover the NT sense of sacrifice and of liturgy. The stress here is on the liturgy of life or, as Ratzinger prefers, cosmic liturgy. The sacrifice to which believers are called is above all the sacrifice of themselves in and with Christ. Related to this is Paul's description in Romans 15:16 of his own preaching of the gospel as a "priestly service." For Ratzinger, as for Conger, Vatican II marked a shift from a narrowly cultic to a more evangelical and missionary understanding of the priesthood.

He returned to Vatican II's view of priesthood in an important article first published in 1968.[7] Although the post-conciliar crisis had already begun it was not so far advanced that he felt the need to respond directly to what was taking place. His treatment is balanced and positive and brings together both biblical and conciliar data.

Ministry in the NT

Renewed biblical scholarship, he says, has destroyed a certain traditional image of the priest as the man of the sacred, set apart to offer a sacrifice of expiation. Such an image has no foundation in the NT and must be "demythologized." Appealing to Hebrews, he emphasizes the radical newness of the NT in comparison with Israel's experience of both priesthood and sacrifice. Cult and holiness are to be understood not in terms of temple worship but in relation to the humanity of Christ. The novelty this represents is reflected in the vocabulary used in the NT for ministry. The language of priesthood is avoided and is replaced by basically profane words like *apostolos, episcopos* and *presbyteros*.

NT practice in this regard tends to be interpreted in two different ways. Some say that the shift in vocabulary is finally unimportant and that the old realities continue under new names. For people with this view, later Catholic developments in regard, for example, to the language of priesthood and the sacramental nature of ordination are more than justified. The opposite view affirms a total break between earlier notions of priesthood and what has become a reality in Christ. *Amt* or office as such no longer exists. What we have are forms of service within the community which, while necessary for the good ordering of it, could be filled by anyone. The priesthood here threatens to become another job, a function that anyone might be called upon to fulfill. It is not necessarily a lifelong vocation nor does it mark its bearers in any decisive and definitive way. Rejecting both alternatives, Ratzinger attempts to find a distinctive approach that will do justice to the concerns that are at least implicitly expressed in them. The pattern of argument that he develops will remain, on the whole, consistent in the future. As its various elements come under attack, he will insist all the more strongly on their validity.

His starting point is christological. If the concept of "office" obviously has an ecclesiological dimension, if it exists in and for the church and can only be exercised in collaboration with all the various charisms and gifts that the Spirit has given to believers, it itself can only be understood in relation to Christ. At the heart of Jesus' self understanding is the notion of mission. He clearly saw himself as someone called and sent by God. He was not appointed "from below," nor was he a representative of those to whom he preached. His life and ministry were lived out in their entirety under a divine "ought."

What was true of Christ was also true of the apostles. Central to Ratzinger's theology of the ministry both in this document and since is his insistence on the apostolate as its key. Where some might underline the uniqueness of the apostolic ministry and develop church ministry more from within the community, he emphasizes the continuity between the two. Although certain aspects of the apostles' ministry, in particular their witness to the resurrection and their role in the original formulation of the gospel, represent a once and for all element in the church's founding, their preaching and pastoral functions continue.

The account of the choosing of the twelve by Jesus is more evocative of the call of prophets than of levites. They are to be with Jesus and to be sent out by him. Both elements remain a part of the church's official ministry. It has a deep religious significance that can only be fulfilled by a personal relationship with Christ in faith and prayer. It is not, however, a monastic vocation. It entails a missionary responsibility, a call to preach the gospel and by doing so to invite people to true worship. Here as in the earlier article Ratzinger insists on the connection between preaching, the eucharist and life. The priest is not set apart except in the sense of being entirely given over to a ministry on behalf of others. A representative of Christ on the one hand, he is called to give himself for others in the service of the gospel. Such a life is only possible in and through Christ. He is not only the model and pattern of ministry, he is present in its activity and alone makes it possible.

Word and Sacrament

Vatican II's recourse to the threefold ministry of prophet, priest, and pastor has to be understood in the light of the underlying unity of ecclesial office. The most basic category here is the word. The community is initially gathered and then renewed and nurtured through preaching. The priest is not primarily a cultic figure but an evangelist. The word that he preaches is not his own, however, but the word of God. True aggiornamento is the bringing of that word into a living relationship with contemporary culture. This, however, can only be accomplished by those who have already done it in their own life.

The priority given to the word in no sense implies a denial of the priest's sacramental responsibilities. Word and sacrament belong together. The eucharist itself is a form of the word; it proclaims and renders present the power for life of the paschal mystery. Pastoral leadership, for its part, must be continually related to and serve the preaching of the gospel. This, Ratzinger suggests, implies a shift in the way pastoral office is to be understood. The categories that should be used here are not "power and authority," but rather "fraternity, love and humanity." The model is Christ the good shepherd.

Augustine's famous phrase, "with you I am a Christian, for you I am a bishop," reveals a fundamental truth about office. It is a relational concept. One becomes a priest for others. Differing responsibilities and ministries do not undermine among believers a fundamental equality in dignity and value.

The medieval notion of the "indelible character" as applied to the ministerial priesthood is rooted in the irreversible nature of God's word and of the Christ event. It also expresses a traditional Catholic conviction about the sacramental nature of ordination. The power that is a part of ecclesial office is not the result of a delegation on the part of the community but rather a gift from the risen Lord in the Spirit. The priest is, as it were, on the side of Christ and represents him in and to the community. The external nature of, and the historical continuity involved in, the laying on of hands corresponds to and reflects the historical and sacramental nature of the Christian revelation. It comes from without, from God. In spite of the presence of grace and of the Spirit in the community, part of the function of the ordained ministry is to give visible expression to the fact that Christ continues to stand over against the church.

There is a secondary sense in which the ordained represent the community but this is limited. The church is not democratic in any of the modern meanings of that word. Office belongs to and makes visible the one ecclesial and christological sacrament, the sacrament of God's once and for all historical covenant with humanity in Christ.

In spite of his overall enthusiasm for PO, Ratzinger does criticize some of its formulations. He finds fault, for example, with its application of Hebrews 5:1 to the presbyterate. The text deals with the OT high priesthood which in Christ has been brought to an end and which in no sense is to be taken up and applied to the NT ministry. In another case he rejects as one-sided and problematic the statement that the presbyter in some sense renders present the bishop in the local liturgical assembly. What the text is positively pointing to is the need for the local pastor and parish to be in genuine communion with the diocese and with and through it and its bishop with the universal church. It is not the bishop but Christ whom the presbyter is to render present in the liturgy.

The Post-Conciliar Crisis

In the late 1960s and then even more in the 1970s and 1980s Ratzinger attempted to respond to the growing crisis in both church and ministry. His episcopal ordination and his move later to Rome as the prefect of the Congregation for the Doctrine of the Faith heightened his sense of responsibility in this regard. He has tended to see the church crisis as part of a larger cultural crisis of western civilization. In analyzing this broader context he has underlined the significance of the shift from the first to the second generation in post-war Europe. The rebuilding was done but in the process the sense of meaning and direction were lost. The student unrest of 1968 was symptomatic. It represented an anarchic and destructive rejection of the emptiness of western materialism. The 1970s and 1980s seemed to be more marked by the triumph of a new middle class with what he describes as individualistic, materialistic, and hedonistic values. Contemporary culture is torn between neo-Marxism and neo-positivism. The result has been a loss of a sense of the metaphysical as well as of the historical. These and other factors have had a considerable impact on the church because of the openness with which church people sought dialogue with the world in the immediate post-conciliar period.

Already in 1965 Ratzinger was critical of Vatican II's Constitution on the Church in the Modern World.[8] He found it insufficiently christocentric, naively optimistic about contemporary culture and above all about the idea of progress, and unclear about the challenge to culture that is a part of the gospel. He believed that the principle of dialogue was undermining evangelization. The writing of the document revealed a division within the progressive forces at the council, a division that would become more marked in the post-conciliar period.

Since the council Ratzinger has been concerned that secularization theology, political theology, and liberation theology in their different ways have tended to reduce the Christian vision of reality to the social betterment of the world. Far from challenging the growing secularity of western culture, such theologies seem to make their own its non-religious character. The result is a loss of the sense of the sacred, an undermining of genuine liturgical worship, and a tendency to see church office in purely functional terms.[9]

It is this functionalization of office against which Ratzinger most strongly reacts. That he does this so vigorously is perhaps due to the misuse that people have made of some of his own earlier emphases. By 1970 he is already lamenting a use of Matthew 23:9 that threatens to undermine the very notion of church structure. More disturbing is the misunderstanding of the NT meaning of *diakonia,* a term that he, like Congar and others, tried to introduce into Catholic reflection on office. The word is now cited as proof that early Christianity knew only a purely functional office. The ordained minister is in no sense the father of the family of God, but simply a functionary with a certain number of tasks to perform. The misuse of *diakonia* in this way is for Ratzinger the crassest example in the history of the church of an authentic NT concept being distorted for ideological purposes.[10] Post-conciliar preoccupation with structure and aggiornamento have contributed to the same effect. They inevitably stress the purely sociological aspects of the church to the detriment of the supernatural, of the realm of mystery. The same concern is at issue in his criticism of certain uses of the language of "people of God."

Reaffirming Vatican II

In response to these developments, he calls for a return to the major emphases of Vatican II, to its sense of church as sacrament and body of Christ, to its use in ecclesiology of the themes of mystery and of communion. Along with Hans Urs von Balthasar he insists on the need for a spiritual and religious renewal and on the indispensable role that saints will have to play in order to bring it about. In his more recent writings he has pleaded for a greater sense of continuity between Old and New Testaments. The priestly and cultic values of Israel are transformed and given new meaning in Christ; they are not simply rejected. Catholics need to rediscover a sense of the sacred, of sacred times and places, of sacred actions, and of sacred persons to preside over them. He defends on occasion the "priestly" interpretation of the ministry but without denying his earlier emphasis on preaching. What is distinctive about the NT priesthood is the fact that it combines both prophetic and priestly qualities. The renewed emphasis on cult is not a justification for a cult in isolation from either the community or the world. Christian cult has a necessary counterpoint in life, a life that truly embodies and reflects the realities celebrated in the liturgy.

Ratzinger attributes some of the difficulties in the inner Catholic discussion of ministry to an inadequate reading of scripture and to a failure to deal with classical problems brought up at the time of the reformation. In regard to the latter, he regrets that some Catholics are tending to cite the Luther of the *Babylonian Captivity* and not the later Luther who in his reaction to the Anabaptists deepened his appreciation of the ministry. Luther's reduction of priesthood to service of the word leads to a functional understanding of office and to an egalitarian view of the church, according to which theoretically anyone could fulfill the tasks of office although for good order only those who are ordained in fact do so.

In reaction Trent insisted on a eucharistic focus for the ministry. The way forward, Ratzinger believes, is not by denying what Trent taught but rather by integrating it into the positive affirmations of the tradition both before and since. This, he continues to believe, is what Vatican II achieved, although its message was either misunderstood or largely abandoned in the post-conciliar period.

Ratzinger's insistence on the eucharist is not a defense of medieval emphases, but rather a way of underlining the continuing significance of the sacraments and especially of the eucharist and of recalling their necessary relationship to both the word and to pastoral leadership. He continues to assert the need to overcome the distinction between orders and jurisdiction. A failure to do so will tend to separate leadership from the sacraments and thus inevitably undermine the sacramental nature of the church.

This kind of conviction makes him initially sympathetic to the claim that a community has a right to the eucharist. His ecclesiology remains in fact eucharistically and liturgically oriented. What he criticizes is not the basic affirmation but the use made of it. The word for community in German in this context is *Gemeinde,* a word which Luther preferred to *Kirche,* which for him smacked of the institutional, the church of pope and bishops. Ratzinger reacts against the tendency in the recent discussion to consider communities more or less in isolation and to see them as providing their own solutions to their needs. In response he insists on the relation among communities and to the church as a whole. Communities and the office that is required to lead them and to preside at their eucharist must be both Catholic and apostolic. The external condition and necessary instrument for assuring that this is indeed the case is episcopal ordination in succession to the apostles.

In recent publications Ratzinger has returned repeatedly to the theme of apostolic succession.[11] It is a necessary and not merely a helpful tool by which the church maintains its connection with the apostolic generation. The historical continuity is accompanied by an ever new and active presence of the Holy Spirit by which successive generations of leaders are endowed with the power and authority to fulfill their ministry in the name and person of Christ. Both elements contribute to establishing the ordained in a position over against the community which in Christ's name they are called to serve. In that "over against," the *extra divinum* (the divine otherness) of biblical revelation is kept alive and made operative.

To Represent Christ

As in his earlier writings Ratzinger continues to stress the christological basis of the ministry. He does not begin with the community and with the various gifts and charisms that the Spirit pours out on it, ready then in a second moment to situate the ordained ministry in relation to them. Whatever the validity of this approach, he is afraid of what in our culture it might lead to. He speaks of a "temptation to pass from that supernatural 'authority of representation,' the hallmark of Catholic priesthood, to a much more natural 'service of the coordination of consensus' . . . more in consonance with modern culture."[12] He seems to see no way of defending against a purely functional, almost secular sense of church office, except by reaffirming its directly christological basis. The ordained are to represent Christ the head who continues to some degree to be over against his body which is the church.

The cardinal argued this point once again in his address to the 1990 Synod of bishops.[13] The foundation of office is to be found in Christ's own mission and in that of the apostles. The gospels recount how in his appointment of the twelve Jesus communicated a share in his ministry to them. In regard to the eucharist and to the forgiveness of sins they are to perform actions that transcend their natural capacities. They will only be able to do so because they have been drawn into the ministry of Jesus. This is what is meant in the church's tradition when it speaks of ordination as a sacrament. It enables a person to act in the person of another, to be his living organ. No community of itself can appoint people to such a ministry. It can only be given from above, from Christ and in the Spirit.

What is true of the twelve is also true of Paul. He clearly distinguishes his ministry from the common pneumatic endowment of all believers. He "acts not out of his own authority but Christ's, not as a member of the community, but as over against the community and as addressing it in Christ's name." The same structure continues in the ministry of the church. Acts 20:26 is said to establish the principle of apostolic succession. Because *presbyteroi* and *episcopoi* are introduced into their ministry by the Holy Spirit, their ordination has the character of a sacrament. They are to continue the "apostolic office of shepherding Christ's flock."[14] Ratzinger finds the same teaching in 1 Peter 5:1–4. Once again the identity of apostolic and presbyteral ministries is affirmed. Both of these texts underline the pastoral nature of office. Because Ratzinger insists on the language of priesthood, he has to conclude that NT priesthood is primarily pastoral.

In the same talk Ratzinger, in contrast to what he was saying at the time of the council, again insists on the continuity between the Old and the New Testaments and on the legitimacy even after Christ of speaking of a ministerial priesthood. It is no more denied by the common priesthood of the faithful than the levitical priesthood was undermined by Israel's status as a priestly people. It would, however, be a distortion of his thought to exaggerate the continuity. The life and death of Jesus entailed a profound transformation in priestly as well as in other categories. This is briefly hinted at here when it is said that "the priesthood of the NT works to the end that the whole world be made a temple and sacrifice acceptable to God so that finally God may be all in all." There is an echo here of his earlier emphasis on the liturgy of life, on cosmic liturgy, an idea that as a young doctoral candidate Ratzinger first met in Augustine's *City of God.*

In recent years, in the course of his many travels, the cardinal has given a number of homilies on the theme of the priesthood. Although not scholarly they do reflect certain theological concerns and convictions.[15] From the above it is not surprising to discover that they are all very much focused on Christ. What Christ says to the twelve or to the intimate group of disciples is said to priests. They are called by him to exercise in regard to others the pastoral office. Theirs is a profoundly religious task, that of leading people to Christ and to God. In order to do so they themselves must know Christ, as it were, at first hand. They must become true disciples and people of prayer. The emphasis is religious, evangelical, Christ-centered. If they are to exercise a ministry, and if in that sense they have a task to perform, they are also called to a way of life. Being must come before doing. Being a priest involves the whole of life and not just isolated moments or specific tasks. It is in this context that Ratzinger defends the traditional demand of the western church for a lifelong commitment on the part of the priest to celibacy.

The images that he uses in the sermons varies somewhat with the different liturgical texts on which he is commenting, but the focus is almost always on word, sacrament, and pastoral leadership. As important as the eucharist is, it is not understood in isolation but as an act of the community, an act that calls those who participate in it to a way of life. To live the eucharist is to enter into Jesus' total "yes" to his Father.

The homilies give one a sense of Ratzinger's theology and also indirectly of those developments in the church about which he is most concerned. Talk of ministries in the plural and of the role of all the faithful, as well as the insistence on the social implications of discipleship have been among the factors in his view which have undermined traditional priestly identity. It is this latter that Ratzinger wants to reinforce, not in the narrow sense that had developed in the medieval and post-Tridentine periods but in a way that does justice to the NT. In spite of certain shifts especially in regard to the language of priesthood, Ratzinger's christocentric and deeply religious concerns, as well as his emphasis on the evangelical and missionary aspect of the Christian priesthood, have remained constant. If anything, the growing secularity of western culture has provoked him to reinforce them.

6

J. Galot: A Pastoral Priesthood

A longtime professor at the Gregorian University and advisor to the Vatican's Congregation for the Clergy, the Belgian Jesuit, Jean Galot, has been a leading figure in post-conciliar debates on the ministerial priesthood. His writings are full of critical references to a wide range of more liberal minded theological colleagues in western Europe, especially in France, Belgium, and Holland. His own positions, laid out initially in a series of articles in various French, Italian, and Spanish publications, were brought together in book form in the 1981 *Teologia del sacerdozio*. The 1985 American translation, *Theology of the Priesthood* (*Priesthood*), has been granted by some members of the American church a quasi-official status.[1] Its publication in English was encouraged and facilitated by the doctrinal committee of the American bishops' conference. It represents a clearly argued and coherent theology that attempts to do justice to Vatican II while reacting vigorously against certain recent developments.

A Christocentric Focus

Galot insists on the theological nature of the ministry and therefore on the inadequacy of a purely sociological approach. It is not enough to reflect on the general need of a community or organization for structure and leadership and then to argue how the church today ought to organize itself. The ministry, like the church, is a divine-human reality given, at least in its essential structure, from above. Not every theological perspective, however, is equally valid. Galot reacts against theologies that take as their exclusive starting point either the church or the Spirit. In opposition to them, he insists on the primacy of Christ. The church is not just any kind of institution, not even just any kind of religious institution. It owes its essential features to Christ. Although these must be adapted to changing situations and needs, they can never be modified in their fundamental nature. The once and for all character of the incarnation is complemented by a strong sense of historical continuity. The church and the ministerial priesthood must remain as Christ intended them until the end of time.

Galot's christocentric perspective on the ministry goes beyond the affirmation that it was instituted by Christ. Jesus was and remains the priest *par excellence,* the ideal embodiment and model of the ministerial priesthood. All priesthood, both that of the faithful and that of the ordained, is a participation, although in quite different ways, in the priesthood of Christ.

Galot does not deny the importance of the Spirit or of the community, but he is anxious to relate both to Christ. Pneumatology and ecclesiology are subordinate to christology. The Spirit that is a part of every Christian life and of every ordination is not just any Spirit but the Spirit of Christ. The church, too, although it is the context within which the ordained are to work, is not the source of their vocation or of their authority. They are called by Christ and endowed with his Spirit in order to exercise his priestly and pastoral power within and to some degree over against the community.

In Galot's judgment the recent emphasis on the functional nature of ministry is the result of an outright denial or at least misunderstanding of traditional teaching on the priestly character. It is this that distinguishes the Catholic understanding of priesthood and that roots it in ontology, in the order of being. If one *is* not something different through ordination, then the ministry is a function that could theoretically be fulfilled by anyone in the community.

As indicated in earlier chapters, a central issue at and after Vatican II had to do with the application to Christian ministry of priestly language. A growing awareness of its absence from the NT raised the question whether it should be used at all in this context and if used how it should be understood. In the 1970s a number of European authors including H. Küng called for its abolition.[2] Galot not only uses it but makes it the central category of his theology of ministry. At first glance this might seem to be a simple return to the post-Tridentine tradition. In fact, however, he gives it a much broader meaning than it had in the pre-Vatican II church.

The Priesthood of Christ

One cannot assume to know *a priori* what "priesthood" means and entails within a specifically Christian context. Neither the history of religions nor the Jewish tradition can provide a normative interpretation. In both cases, although differently, the focus is too narrowly cultic. The Christian priesthood goes back to and is rooted in the person and ministry of Jesus Christ. Galot goes so far as to argue that Jesus consciously inaugurated a new kind of priesthood, one that he intended should be continued in the church. Galot's claims in this regard raise serious questions about his interpretation of the NT. His reading of the gospels and Acts is almost fundamentalist when it comes to issues of historicity. Texts from the synoptics and John, for example, are drawn together almost at random in order to reconstruct the attitude and self-understanding of the historical Jesus. Everything is interpreted in the direction of Galot's general theological perspective and interests. This is particularly true when it comes to the category of priesthood.

Hebrews is the only document in the NT in which Jesus is explicitly called a priest. In fact it refers to him as a high priest on the analogy of the Jewish high priest who once a year on the day of atonement entered into the holy of holies. Jesus fulfills and surpasses the priestly traditions of Israel. He is a priest not of the tribe of Levi and of the house of Aaron, but according to the order of that mysterious priest and king who appears in the story of Abraham, Melchizedek. Hebrews lays out at great length the implications of this affirmation. Other NT writers, especially Paul, while not calling Jesus a priest, interpret aspects of his life and particularly his death in sacrificial terms. The gospels for their part avoid any explicitly priestly language in their presentations of Jesus.

On the basis of the developed theology of Hebrews, Galot

believes himself justified in claiming that Jesus had a priestly consciousness and that he saw himself embodying and inaugurating a
priesthood different from and superior to the Jewish priesthood.
Although Jesus does not call himself a priest, Galot argues that
certain texts indicate that this was the way he thought about himself. The stories of the cleansing of the temple and especially the
word of Jesus about its being destroyed and then rebuilt suggest
something of this nature. Said to be even more conclusive is Jesus'
response to the high priest during the passion story. Reading the
entire trial as a confrontation between the two priesthoods, Galot
sees its climax in the question of the high priest whether Jesus is the
Messiah, the Son of God. The phrase in Jesus' answer, "the Son of
Man seated at the right hand of power and coming on the clouds of
heaven," evokes Psalm 110. The psalmist relates this sitting at the
right hand of God to being a priest according to the order of
Melchizedek. For Galot the conclusion is obvious: "Jesus, then,
claims the eternal priesthood attributed to the Messiah. . . . Before the high priest and his colleagues, Jesus declares that they will
see the advent of this new priesthood on the clouds of heaven."
(37)

Galot stresses that the priesthood of Jesus represents a radical
break from the priesthood of Israel. It is a spiritual and personal
priesthood whose purpose is to build up a community of faith and
love. Christian priesthood in all its forms involves consecration and
mission. Because in Jesus the consecration is rooted in the incarnation, he belongs in a totally unique way to the world of the sacred;
"he is the sacred man *par excellence.*" (38) Never merely functional, the priesthood always has implications for the being of the
priest; it involves "a way of life," in Italian *un stato di vita.* It is
ontological in nature. Inseparable, however, from consecration is
mission. In Christ and in the church priesthood does not mean
separation except for greater involvement; it has a dynamic quality
that is ordered to the salvation of the world.

Priest as Pastor

Turning to the actual content of Jesus' mission, Galot stresses
his pastoral activity. Jesus is the good shepherd sent from God to

gather the lost sheep of Israel. He does this by his teaching, example, and the sacrifice of his life. For Galot the Christian use of the language of sacrifice as well as of priesthood comes less from the world of Jewish cult than from the nature of Jesus' mission as the shepherd. Laying down his life for his sheep, he offers the sacrifice that brings forgiveness and constitutes authentic worship.

While highlighting the pastoral authority and power of Jesus, Galot insists that what is distinctive about his mission is that he exercises it as a service, a *diakonia*. As Mark 10:45 puts it, he came not to be served but to serve and to give his life as a ransom for the many. For Galot as for Ratzinger and Congar, priesthood, in Jesus, no longer belongs to the world of things and of external cult but to the realm of the person and of love. His life as shepherd is a service, a sacrifice of self-giving love, a ministry. Here we have not only a transformation of the traditional notion of priesthood, but a model for all future exercises of "pastoral power." In Jesus "priesthood has become service, that is, ministry. It is this principle of priestly authority exercised as a service that constitutes the ideal of ministry which the disciples must try to live." (45)

Like many others, Galot refers to the threefold ministry of Christ as priest, prophet and king. What distinguishes his approach is the conviction that the unifying element among the three is the pastoral one. It includes teaching, sacrifice and leadership. This, finally, is what sets off Jesus' understanding of the priesthood from that of the OT. Whereas it tended to restrict priesthood "to the domain of worship, the shepherd takes on the function of the prophet, of the priest in the cultic sense, and of the king, all at the same time." (49)

If the priesthood of Jesus is the first and key element in Galot's theology of the priesthood, the apostolic ministry also plays a crucial part. Some aspects of it are unique, while others will be continued in the life of the church. The presentation begins with the twelve and with their "institution" by Jesus. In the phrase "he made them twelve" one can discern a reference to creation and to the establishment of a new being. That they are to be with Jesus before being sent out on their mission is to be interpreted in the strongest sense possible. The establishment of the twelve has ontological implications: priestly activity flows from priestly being. The interrelation of consecration and mission applies to the apostles as much as to Jesus. In fact almost everything that is said of Jesus' priesthood can be said of their priesthood as well, for by definition it is a participation in his priesthood. He entrusted to them his own mission and the power to fulfill it, the power to teach authoritatively, to forgive sins, to preside at the eucharist, to govern and structure the community. As in the case of Jesus, their pastoral power is to be exercised as a service, a *diakonia*. The model and ontological basis of this is Jesus' own act of self-giving love.

Although he mentions the last supper and insists that it was only the twelve who received the command on that occasion to celebrate the eucharist, Galot does not, like John Paul II and Trent, identify that command with an act of ordination. This he sees as involving a number of moments including the various charges that Jesus made to the twelve during his life, the imposition of hands suggested in Luke 24:50, and the coming of the Spirit at Pentecost. (156f) As priests, the apostles stand to some degree on the side of Christ over against the church. Through word, sacrament, and pastoral leadership they exercise an office of mediation; through them "the Christian community will achieve union with Christ." (74) They are neither chosen by nor represent the community but are called and ordained by Christ and are given a share in his pastoral office.

Ministry as Priesthood

What is true of the apostles is to a large degree true of the priesthood within the church. In much of what he has to say here Galot makes no distinction between bishops and presbyters. For him as for most theologians today the two terms are interchangeable in the NT. It was only later that the hierarchy as we now know it developed. He affirms and makes his own the shift that Vatican II represents in this regard in comparison with Trent. The fundamental office is the episcopate in which in a restricted sense the presbyterate shares.

In his reading of the NT Galot emphasizes elements of continuity between the apostles and post-apostolic forms of ministry. He claims that succession in the ministry was a concern of Jesus himself. The mission entrusted to the apostles was an enduring one that needed to be handed on to successors. "Jesus willed a succession marked by historical continuity with himself and with the group of the Twelve. . . . We should never think that, as the Church develops, the Holy Spirit might one day break in to confer, in charismatic fashion, a priestly ministry historically unrelated to the first apostles through succession. . . . He bestows the priestly power only through a chain of historical transmission in which the Twelve are the first link." (87)

Like the ministry of Christ and the apostles, the ordained ministry within the church is understood primarily in terms of priesthood. As with them, the use of the word priesthood here suggests not only functional but also ontological implications. In traditional theology this kind of claim has been associated with the doctrine of "the priestly character." Although a number of recent authors have denied it any dogmatic status, Galot maintains that it was defined as part of Catholic dogma at Trent. Baptism, confirmation, and orders all imprint a "character," a spiritual and indelible mark that configures the person to Christ. Although not a "thing," it is a reality that modifies the being of those who receive it in the sense of consecrating them to God in Christ. Through the baptismal character and the gift of the Spirit people share in the being of Christ, including his priesthood. What is distinctive of the character given in orders is not that it makes a person another Christ or that it configures someone to him for the first time, but rather that it consecrates someone to Christ the shepherd. It gives the ordained a share in Christ's pastoral priesthood and enables them to act within the community in the name and with the power of the risen Christ.

To stress the ontological aspect of the priestly character is not to deny its functional implications. It is a dynamic reality that pushes to action. The priesthood belongs to the order of doing as well as of being. Galot insists on both even while giving a certain priority to the latter. "If the priest is to be capable of doing God's work, he must belong to God with his whole self. It is not in vain that he is called not merely God's messenger, but the man of God." (202) The attempt to "demystify" the character implies a denial that priesthood involves any special configuration to Christ or that it demands a particular way of life; it reduces it to a mere function that ultimately anyone within the community could fulfill.

Pastoral Leadership

When it comes to spelling out in more detail the tasks involved in the ministerial priesthood, Galot has recourse to the three traditional functions highlighted at Vatican II. Rather than simply juxtapose them, however, he asks whether they cannot be unified. Unlike Congar and Rahner he refuses to take either sacrifice or the word as the key. Even leadership, if understood in terms of governance and administration, is unable to function as a unifier. The crucial element is "the quality of shepherd" as lived by Jesus. With him and with the ministers of the church, "it is the shepherd's quality that best epitomizes the priestly function." (137) Central to it is the exercise of authority, an authority that comes to the priest in virtue of his ordination and by which he is made a sharer in Christ's own pastoral office. This is an authority of love and service, an authority that is given in order to build up and lead the community. It entails preaching and teaching as well as presiding at the eucharist.

In embracing a radically pastoral understanding of the ministerial priesthood Galot consciously moves beyond the perspective of Trent. Although its teaching cannot be denied, it can be integrated into a larger and more balanced whole. This he sees as the primary contribution of Vatican II. To put it most simply, as important as the eucharist is, presiding at it "cannot be isolated from the entire pastoral mission. It must be regarded as the apex of the pastoral task which is meant to serve the community and provide leadership." (141)

In spite of his idiosyncratic claims about the consciousness Jesus had of establishing a new "priesthood," it is clear from his emphasis on the pastoral dimension of the ministry that Galot's main concern is not the category of priesthood, but rather the connection of the church's ministry with Christ. This connection is direct and not mediated by the community. It involves both historical and vertical dimensions. The former is related to the notion of apostolic succession, while the later recalls the ever new empowerment of the ordained by the risen Lord through the Spirit. It is Christ who calls his ministers and who gives them a share in his pastoral power so that they can act in his name. They are his representatives and in some sense sacraments of his continuing concern for his people. Configured in a special way to Christ, the priest is and is called to be a man of the sacred, a man of God. The priesthood is forever and demands of those who receive it a way of life that sets them apart from the laity as a whole. As much as priests are to be concerned about people and about their spiritual well-being, their focus should be a religious one.

Galot's theology of the priesthood contains much that is in Vatican II but it tends to emphasize those aspects of the conciliar teaching that many in the post-conciliar period were neglecting. It reacts against the secular and democratic concerns of the late 1960s and the widespread tendency in the 1970s and later to emphasize the functional aspect of ministry. It represents to some degree the opposite extreme of those who see the ministry and ministries from an ecclesiological and pneumatological perspective. From beginning to end his view of the priesthood is radically christocentric. Although he goes well beyond the traditional understanding of the language of priesthood, he insists on making it central to his presentation. This may be simply out of respect for the Catholic tradition or it may represent a desire to combat the secularizing trend of contemporary western culture.

7
Schillebeeckx and His Critics

Born in Belgium in 1914, Edward Schillebeeckx, O.P. has been involved in and influenced many of the efforts at theological and pastoral renewal in the Roman Catholic Church over the last forty years. Present at Vatican II as a peritus, he contributed to its formulations especially in the areas of ecclesiology, sacraments, and the relation between the church and the world. In the post-conciliar period his theology took a new turn in its acceptance of the hermeneutical and other challenges arising out of modern Protestant and secular thought and in its increased focus on issues of culture, politics, and liberation. A necessary prerequisite to his massive reworking of traditional christology was his openness to modern NT criticism.[1]

Although best known for his books on christology, Schille-beeckx both before and after the council wrote a number of articles on the ordained ministry or on what he, like his German colleagues, tends to call ecclesial "office." Since the late 1960s these writings have been influenced as much by the actual situation of the church and of priests, especially in Holland where he began teaching in 1958, as by scholarly interests. In 1980 he issued four of these articles together with other material in book form. Published in an American translation in 1981 as *Ministry: Leadership in the Community of Jesus Christ* (*Ministry*), the work provoked considerable though varied reaction.[2] While some welcomed it enthusiastically, many European theologians, and not just the most conservative, criticized it from a variety of viewpoints. The Vatican Congregation for the Doctrine of the Faith (CDF) launched an investigation and published a letter in 1984, signed by Cardinal Ratzinger, that was critical of several points in it.

Partly in response to criticism, Schillebeeckx issued in 1985 a second book, translated into English as *The Church with a Human Face: A New and Expanded Theology of Ministry (Human Face).*[3] It contained much of *Ministry* together with some additions and changes. Although it was greeted positively by some who had criticized the earlier work, the CDF again judged it to contain positions incompatible with the Catholic faith.

Given the lively and continuing debate provoked by the two books, they will form the focus of the present chapter. It will also include some indication of the major criticisms they have encountered. At the outset it is perhaps important to point out that the use of the English word "ministry" in the title and throughout the first book has been a source of some confusion. The original Dutch title is *Kerkelijk Ambt,* literally, ecclesial office. Like the German *Amt,* the Dutch word has a narrower focus than ministry as currently used in North America. It suggests an institutionalized reality, something of an official and therefore ecclesially recognized nature. The broader use of "ministry" is normally expressed in the book by the word "service."

Alternative Practices

Although *Ministry* contains a good deal of biblical and historical material, its focus is not exegetical or historical scholarship. Schillebeeckx writes as a theologian and he writes with a concrete pastoral situation in view. His starting point is the contemporary church and in particular the church in Holland. The situation there is marked on the one hand by a growing shortage of priests and on the other by the spread of what he variously refers to as grass roots or critical communities. These have given birth to "alternative practices," which while not spelled out seem to involve communities without priests appointing one of their own members to act as leader and to preside at the eucharist.

The intent of the book is not simply or even primarily to legitimate such practices, but rather to test them in the light both of tradition and of the gospel. To do this it is not sufficient to recall the definitions of Trent or even of Vatican II. Conciliar statements have to be situated within the whole history of Christian experience of, and reflection on, the ordained ministry. It is only within this context that one can discern in so historically conditioned a reality what reflects authentic theological insight and what is the result of non-theological factors. The exposition is structured around a fundamental shift that sets off the second millennium of church history from the first. In a related but somewhat subordinate way, the book also speaks of three forms of ecclesial office: the ancient, the medieval, and the modern. The last, largely identified with post-Tridentine developments, remained in force up to Vatican II. The present struggle and conflict may well herald the birth of a fourth form.

The book begins with a fairly substantial chapter on the NT. As much as biblical scholars might argue about individual points of interpretation, the method and the general results reflect the approach of contemporary critical exegesis. The treatment of the NT material could hardly be more different from that of Galot. For Schillebeeckx little of church order can be traced back to the historical Jesus. He also emphasizes the distinction between the apostolic and post-apostolic ages. If the local churches saw themselves as committed to the apostolic teaching and to the way of life it implied, leadership within them was at least in part a spontaneous development. There was a widespread sense of the presence of the Spirit and of the rich variety of his gifts. Those who were specially gifted assumed positions of leadership. Some were probably appointed by the founding apostles while others came to be recognized and accepted by the communities themselves.

In the first decades there was no common terminology for these leaders. They were variously called *presbyteroi* or elders, *episcopoi* or overseers, pastors, teachers or even leaders. Within the NT there is no clear indication of what later will be called the "monarchical episcopate." By the time of the pastorals there is a real preoccupation with organizing and institutionalizing the various ministries. By the same time the practice of laying on of hands seems to be the norm, although according to Schillebeeckx it is not clear that it ever became a universal and therefore necessary practice within the NT period.

Community Leadership

Initially the focus was not on the eucharist and on the power in virtue of which someone presides at it, but rather on community leadership. Those who were recognized and publicly accepted as leaders naturally led the community at the eucharist as they did at all its official gatherings. Within the NT the emphasis is on preaching, admonition, and pastoral care. The notion of apostolicity is primarily a characteristic of the community. The ministry is at the service of the apostolic tradition and of the apostolicity of the whole church. The emphasis everywhere is on roles or functions and not on any kind of ontology that would separate the minister from other believers. There is no division in the NT between clergy and laity.

Given his contemporary concerns, it is not surprising that Schillebeeckx insists on the right of a community, by grace, to leadership and to the eucharist. Both in virtue of sociological laws and by the will of Christ, the community for its own survival and development needs to have adequate leadership as well as the possibility of celebrating its most fundamental rituals. The present shortage of priests, he argues, would have been simply incomprehensible to the NT mentality.

Unlike Ratzinger and Galot, Schillebeeckx is not concerned to attach the developing church ministries directly to Jesus and to his institution of the twelve. While recognizing that presbyters and overseers continue certain aspects of the leadership of the apostles, he sees the growth of church office as a result of basic sociological laws of community development. In this sense NT ministries are not directly given "from above" but arise "from below." Since the community, however, is the body of Christ and is animated by the Holy Spirit, this sociological "from below" is at the same time, to the eyes of faith, "from above." A major concern of Schillebeeckx in the book is to overcome what he perceives as an ecclesiological dualism or false "supernaturalism," that is, an artificial separation between a recognition of the concrete conditions under which communities develop and a theological interpretation of their final religious significance.

The First Millennium

Throughout the first millennium the understanding of the ministry was primarily pneumatological and ecclesiological. Once the "monarchical episcopate" became the norm, the focus was on the leadership responsibilities of the bishop. His presiding at the eucharist followed from, and was implied in, his leadership role. To make his point Schillebeeckx appeals to the sixth canon of the Council of Chalcedon and to the early liturgical tradition, especially as contained in the *Apostolic Tradition* of Hippolytus. The fact that the Chalcedonian canon declared absolute ordinations invalid underlines the widespread early church conviction that ministry is a service in and for the community. The same view lies behind the practice of ministers returning to the lay state if for whatever reason they can or will no longer fulfill their assigned office. On this and on a number of other historical points Schillebeeckx grounds his argument on positions arrived at by the patristic scholar C. Vogel. His work figures frequently in recent literature on the ministerial priesthood. While some authors accept and build on what he says, others, like Joseph Lécuyer in *Le Sacrement de l'ordination* (Paris, 1983), find elements of it tendentious.

Schillebeeckx distinguishes between the appointment of people to office and the rite of the laying on of hands. The two almost always coexist, but theologically the first is more significant. "In the first millennium, both in the East and in the West, the necessity for the laying on of hands at the *ordinatio* of ministers was strongly relativized; recognition and sending by the community is the really decisive element. . . . The history of the first millennium therefore leaves completely open the question whether the rite of consecration is absolutely necessary." (*Ministry* 47)

Schillebeeckx refers, as Congar and others have, to the absence of priestly language for the ministry in the NT. When it began to be used at the end of the second century, it still did not imply any particular emphasis on the eucharist. People became leaders of the church and as such presided at the liturgy. There was, moreover, a widely held sense that presbyters and bishops did not offer the eucharist for the community but rather with it. Schillebeeckx speaks here of "concelebration" and concludes enigmatically: "so in the early church the eucharist could always take place when the community met together." (50)

In a closely related section he asks whether a lay person could preside at the eucharist. Basing himself largely on a single text of Tertullian he argues that in the pre-Nicean church "in exceptional circumstances the community itself chose its president *ad hoc.*" (51) Whatever the case of such exceptions, the main point made in regard to the first millennium is that during it ministry was seen as primarily related not to the eucharist and a sacred power in virtue of which the priest is able to consecrate it, but rather to pastoral leadership, a leadership which naturally included presiding at the liturgy. It is above all on this point that the contrast is made between the first and second millennia.

The Second Millennium

Although the change did not take place all at once, Schillebeeckx sees indications of a new emphasis in the decrees of the Third and Fourth Lateran Councils. The ecclesial nature of the ministry begins to fade, and the priesthood becomes progressively more privatized. Through ordination a person receives the power to confect the eucharist and to perform sacramental actions. There is a shift from the church to the eucharist and from pastoral leadership to sacramental power. A number of factors seem to have been at work in this process including the feudal order of society, the existence of private churches in the hands of wealthy landowners, and above all the resurgence of Roman law with its fostering of the distinction between the power of orders and the power of jurisdiction. This last factor facilitated the multiplication of private masses and the appearance of so-called mass-saying priests.

Although many recent scholars have attributed the shifts that took place in the practice and understanding of the ministry at this time to the development of a theology of the priestly "character," Schillebeeckx is more nuanced in his reading of what happened.

The theology of character developed by the great scholastics continued, in fact, to emphasize the priest's relationship to the community. In regard, moreover, to its ontological status, they differed
sharply among themselves. It was only later that their speculations
"would contribute to an ontological and even magical sacerdotalizing of the priesthood." (55) Here briefly in his own words is
Schillebeeckx's view of what took place. In the medieval period "a
priest is ordained in order to be able to celebrate the eucharist; in
the ancient church it is said that he is 'appointed' as minister in
order to be able to appear as leader of the community; in other
words, the community called him as leader to build up the community, and for this reason he was also the obvious person to preside
at the eucharist. This shift is of the utmost importance: at all
events, it is a narrower legalistic version of what the early church
believed." (58)

Within the second millennium Schillebeeckx distinguishes between two different forms of the priesthood, the medieval and the
modern. The latter he sees taking shape in the writings of Josse
Clichtove (1472–1543) who emphasized the priestly interpretation
of the ministry and appealed to the OT levitical model for ideas
about how it should be both understood and lived. Here the priest
is above all the man of the cult, the religious person set apart from
the world, including the world of the laity, in order to offer sacrifice on behalf of others. Clichtove is anxious to develop a theology
and spirituality for the large number of priests who were ordained
but who exercised no pastoral responsibilities. For him, "priesthood is less an office than a state, grounded in cultic activity." (59)
It is at this time that the image of the priest becomes "completely
clerical, hierarchical and monastic." (60) As positive as Clichtove's
efforts were to enhance the spiritual life of the priest, the result
was one-sided. "The image of the priest as the solitary private
sayer of 'masses' without further pastoral responsibilities, took on
a certain divine aura." (60)

While avoiding the excesses of Clichtove, Trent's doctrinal
statement on the ministry was also one-sided. Its emphasis was on
priesthood and on the power given through ordination to confect
the eucharist and to forgive sins. The fact of an indelible character
is affirmed although nothing is said about its specific nature.

Preaching and pastoral responsibilities are mentioned in the reform decrees, but these unfortunately were largely forgotten in the course of the development of what is known as the Tridentine model of the priesthood. Based on the doctrinal affirmations of Trent, it took on concrete and persuasive form in the spirituality and formation program of the French school of the seventeenth and eighteenth centuries. Through the Sulpicians in particular these had wide influence throughout the church and formed the basis for the view at the heart of the major documents on the priesthood of the twentieth century papacy.

Recent Developments

Against this background the effort of Vatican II to relate the presbyterate to the episcopate, and to understand both in terms of their pastoral responsibilities, represented a significant step forward. It marked a rediscovery of some of the emphases of the patristic period. The result, however, was not a totally integrated vision. Elements of the modern view of the priest remained, ready to be appealed to and focused on in the post-conciliar period.

Schillebeeckx is particularly negative about the 1971 synod of bishops. The crisis of the late 1960s was leading some people to approach the issue of priesthood and ministry from a pragmatic and sociological perspective. This provoked a "supernaturalist" reaction. The failure of the synod was rooted in its inability to overcome the growing polarization between "two powerful extremes, 'supernaturalism' (and 'fideism') on the one hand, and horizontalism on the other." (106) Taking an almost exclusively religious perspective, the former sees the issues in terms of Christ's call and gifts and the priest's response and commitment. The latter tends to view the ministry as a profession with little sensitivity to its religious depth. For Schillebeeckx the failure to resolve this tension prevented the synod from dealing with the growing crisis of the clergy and led it to make affirmations that fall short of the positions of Vatican II. The synod, like the 1976 Declaration on the Ordination of Women after it, represents a narrowly christological as opposed to a pneumatological and ecclesial view of office.

In a final section Schillebeeckx turns to what had been his

starting point, the "alternative practices" of grass roots communities. Although these are clearly *praeter ordinem,* outside current canonical regulations, they are not finally, in his mind, *contra ordinem,* against these regulations in their deepest meaning. He is able to hold this because of his reading of history. It suggests that the critical issue in regard to the ministry is pastoral leadership and that the key to it is the recognition and/or acceptance of a leader by a community. The actual laying on of hands, while important, is secondary. For Schillebeeckx, the right of a community to the eucharist outweighs any canonical requirement that the church might make for ordination.

The fact that some communities are designating one of their own members to preside at the eucharist raises serious questions that need to be addressed. Schillebeeckx sees what is happening as having a diagnostic and critical significance as well as, in some sense, a normative one. The practice underlines the gravity of the shortage of priests and questions the continuing validity of current canonical norms. It suggests that the modern understanding of the priest has become an ideology that no longer corresponds to the needs of the church and the world. The ideology is focused on the "character," at least as this came to operate in post-Tridentine theology and spirituality. Understood in an "ontological and sacerdotalist" way, it isolates the priest from the community and seems to demand celibacy and to prevent the possibility of ordaining women.

Instead of simply rejecting the notion of the character as some would, Schillebeeckx interprets it as "the charisma of ministry [which] is given as a function [or] a service to the community, a service which in fact requires complete personal dedication from the one who is called through 'the community of God.' " (127) Such an understanding underlines the ecclesial and pneumatic aspects of office and, if accepted, would free church authorities to be more creative in their response to present pastoral needs. "A concern for what we can conveniently call the 'modern, Tridentine view of the priest' is scarcely an expression of concern for the actual living apostolic vitality of a creative Christian community." (142)

As already suggested, the book provoked strong reactions both positive and negative, and that among different groups and in a variety of countries. Many greeted with enthusiasm its reading of history and its apparent legitimation of the "alternative practices" of critical communities. Among those who were critical, some focused on aspects of its biblical and historical interpretation, while others reacted to its theological positions and/or its practical implications.

Critical Reactions

Jean Galot stands for many in his fundamentally negative response.[4] The notion that the priesthood as a participation in the priesthood of Christ confers a sacred power enabling the priest to act in the name of Christ was always a part of the church's understanding and not a product of the second millennium. Schillebeeckx's approach, in Galot's judgment, is vitiated by a fundamental "prejudice" according to which the ministry is seen as "an autonomous product of the community." The claim that the local community has the power to call its own ministers and in a case of necessity to appoint them to preside at the eucharist "is contrary to the doctrine of the ministerial priesthood instituted by Christ and confided to the universal church." Schillebeeckx in *Ministry* "abandons the faith of the church."

Albert Vanhoye, S.J., a longtime professor at the Biblical Institute in Rome, focuses his lengthy review on the chapter on the NT.[5] While admitting that there is much there with which he can agree, he is extremely critical about the presentation on apostles and apostolicity. In accounting for the development of local church structures the text minimizes the role of the apostles and exaggerates the place of spontaneity. Vanhoye sees no reason to doubt that the apostles and those who cooperated with them in the founding of churches took an active role in the appointment of local leaders. The downplaying of the apostles leads to a distortion of the notion of apostolicity. While emphasizing the apostolic nature of the whole church and the role of scripture and tradition in relation to it, the book fails to do justice to apostolic succession in the ministry. A further result of the same disregard is the emphasis on the development of ministry "from below." This denies the clear NT witness to the appointment of the twelve by Jesus and to the importance of the resurrection experiences in the establishment of the apostolic office. Vanhoye rejects the formulation about the "right" of communities to the eucharist and to leadership as simply foreign to the NT context.

The longest response to *Ministry* is a 250-page book by the French exegete Pierre Grelot.[6] Although focusing on the NT material, it ranges widely and touches on a number of theological and pastoral issues. Grelot's most general criticism is of methodology. He sees the preoccupation with critical communities and their practices as not simply directing but distorting the reading of the NT and of history. Like Vanhoye, Grelot believes that Schillebeeckx has not done justice to the NT understanding of apostolicity. The apostles not only preached, they established an institutional structure, the development of which within the NT period is normative. A hypothetical reconstruction of the church order known by the Matthean community, for example, is not to be played off against that of Acts and the pastoral epistles.

Grelot broaches some of the larger issues in the debate, where, in spite of a critical tone, he reveals himself on most points to be much closer to Schillebeeckx than, for example, to Galot. This is particularly true in his handling of "priesthood." He describes the universal priesthood as ontological and the priesthood of the ordained as functional. The minister is at the service of Christ, prophet, pastor and priest. In presiding at the eucharist he serves the priestly act of Christ in his unique sacrifice which through the sacrament is rendered present in the midst of the community. It is finally Christ who presides at the eucharist, but through the visible and functional service of the minister. Understood in this functional sense, priestly language can be applied to the ministry, but it is open to misunderstanding. This is what happened in the French school with its excessively sacerdotalizing and narrowly cultic approach. The Christian priest is not a man apart, a man of the sacred, not a priest in any ordinary sense of that word. A witness of the gospel, he has accepted the responsibility for the life of the community and on that basis is charged to preside at the eucharist. Where Grelot differs from Schillebeeckx is in the emphasis that he gives to the apostolic succession of bishops and to its necessity for continuity in the ministry.

In *The Church with a Human Face* Schillebeeckx affirms his gratitude to H. Crouzel, a patristic scholar, for his criticism of historical detail.[7] Among the specific points with which he and others found fault are the interpretation of 1 Clement, the dating of Ignatius, the recourse to Tertullian to argue for lay people presiding at the eucharist, the reading of Cyprian's use of priestly language as allegorical, the meaning of concelebration in the early church, the precise meaning of canon 6 of Chalcedon, the history including the motivation for celibacy, and the concern in early canonical regulations to assure in the election of bishops the role both of the local community and of neighboring bishops. This last issue is central to Crouzel's criticism of Schillebeeckx's reading of early church history. The appointment of bishops is not simply or even primarily a matter of the local community. There is also the question of "apostolic succession." "A bishop is made by the coming together of both elements. To disregard one of them is to distort the institutions of the primitive church. The gift of the Spirit comes from both elements and not just from the community." (740)

Walter Kasper's criticisms are more theological.[8] They focus on four points, the first of which is the issue of a christological and/or a pneumatological basis for ecclesial office. For Kasper, Schillebeeckx's focus on the pneumatic and ecclesial aspects fails to do justice to the NT emphasis on Christ and on the continuing presence of Christ through word and ministry in and over against the community. A second point of criticism is the insistence on the functional nature of office. Relating this to the Augustine/Donatist controversy, Kasper accuses Schillebeeckx of furthering a "purely charismatic" view of church and ministry. The rejection of an ontological understanding is interpreted as a rejection of the idea that through the ministry the risen Christ continues to act in the church.

A third point has to do with the emphasis put on the appointment of a minister by the community. This seems to Kasper to imply that in the end priests are not only ordained for communities but by them. This same point comes back in regard to the issue whether a non-ordained person can preside at the eucharist. Kasper argues that the ecclesial nature of the eucharist demands that it only be celebrated in harmony and communion with the whole church and with its bishops. In this sense, a community that would appoint someone to celebrate the eucharist without that person's being ordained would be positing a self-contradictory act. Far from recapturing an authentic tradition of the early church, Schillebeeckx's proposal tends to a Free Church position.

A more nuanced and yet not uncritical review was offered by Congar.[9] Anyone, he says, who wanted to criticize Schillebeeckx's thesis on the basis of the theology of the presbyterate that came out of scholasticism and Trent would have little trouble doing so. If, however, one were to read these developments, as one should, within the whole of church history, then criticism becomes more difficult. Granting this, Congar still raises a number of questions. The first is whether the distinction made between the appointment and reception of ministers and their ordination does not undermine the value of ordination and its sacramental reality. Another question asks whether the difference between the first and second millennia has been exaggerated. The call for a return to the first, moreover, should include an effort to integrate what is authentic in the second.

A third question has to do with the danger of undermining unity by stressing the independent role of local communities, while a fourth touches on a number of historical interpretations some of which have been cited above. Congar concludes with an affirmation that Schillebeeckx's questions and challenges must be taken seriously. Communities have a right to the eucharist, and if present canonical dispositions prevent the ordination of a sufficient number of ministers to meet the needs, then "these dispositions must be changed." Schillebeeckx's work "can be criticized; it should be neither disregarded nor suppressed."

The CDF initiated an exchange with Schillebeeckx in order, as it put it, to clarify certain positions taken in the book. On June 13, 1984, Cardinal Ratzinger, the prefect of the Congregation, sent a letter to Schillebeeckx laying out its final judgment.[10] The letter's critical remarks focus on the possibility of what it calls "ministers extraordinary" of the eucharist. Although the phrase appears only peripherally in *Ministry,* Schillebeeckx had used it in his correspondence with the CDF. The term was obviously chosen because of an analogous and earlier use of it in relation to baptism and confirmation. The letter rejects it and with it the possibility of a celebration of the eucharist by anyone not ordained in the apostolic succession of the bishops. Because Schillebeeckx had claimed that the question was an open one, the CDF issued a document dated August 6, 1983 on the topic under the title *Sacerdotium ministeriale*.[11] It reaffirmed the teaching of Trent and Vatican II about the need of episcopal or presbyteral ordination in order to celebrate the eucharist and affirmed that to claim the contrary "undermines the entire apostolic structure of the church and distorts the sacramental economy of salvation itself." Ordination not only confers "apostolic powers," it also confers a character in virtue of which Christ configures the ordained to himself so that they are able to pronounce the words of consecration *in persona Christi*. Even the most extraordinary of circumstances cannot justify a bypassing of this requirement.

In his letter to Schillebeeckx, Ratzinger appeals to this document to justify his claim that the issue of "ministers extraordinary" of the eucharist is not an "open question" and that "the last word" has indeed been spoken by the magisterium. He concludes by asking Schillebeeckx to declare his acceptance of the teaching of *Sacerdotium ministeriale*. In a letter to the cardinal of November 1984, Schillebeeckx refers to the soon to appear *Human Face* and affirms that in it "there is nothing to be found . . . which contradicts the Congregation's declaration of 6 August 1983 regarding the *sacerdotium ministeriale*. In the hope of avoiding from now on all misunderstanding, the theme of apostolic succession has been analyzed more fully."[12]

Schillebeeckx Responds

The Church with a Human Face: A New and Expanded Theology of Ministry was published in 1985, the same year as the original Dutch edition, the literal translation of the title of which reads: *A Plea for Human Beings in the Church: Christian Identity and Offices in the Church*. The author says he wrote the second book partly in order to respond to criticisms, some of which, including those of Kasper, Grelot, and the CDF, were in his judgment based, in part at least, on misunderstanding. About seventy-five percent of *Ministry* is included in the new book although the material is distributed in a somewhat different way and at a number of points is corrected. Almost twice as long as the first book, *Human Face* includes a much expanded and more nuanced presentation of the historical material. Entirely new is Part One which offers a summary overview of the preaching and destiny of Jesus and of the beginnings of the first communities of faith. What is said here reflects the christology developed in the *Jesus* and *Christ* books.

Equally new is the first section of Part Two which deals with the growth of leadership within the early church, but primarily from a socio-historical point of view. A second section contains the NT material from *Ministry*, material that is now described as primarily theological. The existence of the new section reveals what is clearly a growing conviction: a merely theological approach to ministry is bound to be ideological. Authority, leadership, and institutional structures are historical realities developing and changing in response to situations both inside and outside the church. The theological significance of the ministry can only be discussed after a serious historical analysis of its concrete forms. It is in vain that one tries to distill a simple theological content from the changing forms. Efforts in this direction reflect a false "supernaturalism."

Beyond this general point, the actual treatment of material reveals a radical vision of the origins of ministry. The focus is on pre-Pauline, Pauline, and post-Pauline developments. Following E. Schüssler Fiorenza and other exegetes he argues that initially these communities were marked by a sense of fundamental equality. "Early Christianity was a brotherhood and sisterhood of equal partners: theologically on the basis of the baptism of the Spirit, and sociologically in accordance with the Roman Hellenistic model for free societies, called *collegia.*" (*Human Face* 47) Very soon and in an effort to live at peace with the dominant contemporary culture, it took on the hierarchical thinking of the Greco-Roman household "with its explicit aspects of androcentrism, power and subjection." (69) In this sense the situation in the pastorals and Ephesians already represents a fall away from the original ideal. The same time frame witnessed a shift not so much from charism to institution as from the many charisms to the one charism of the developing office. Typical here was the gradual appropriation by local leadership of the doctrinal authority of the earlier prophets and teachers. In the second century the process will go a step further when the role of presbyters will be subsumed by bishops.

Important for Schillebeeckx's overall theological position is his conclusion "that originally there were times when ministry in the church was exercised on the basis of the baptism of the Spirit, the pneumatic power of which was manifested more clearly in certain believers than in others." (73) The theological issue that this raises is "the relationship of the baptism of the Spirit (*sacramentum baptismi* . . .) to the spiritual charisms of ministry (*sacramentum ordinis*)." The pursuit of this theme is the most striking new element in his reworking of the NT material from *Ministry*. One of the conclusions of this section is precisely that "what is later rightly called *sacramentum ordinis* is a specific, viz. diaconal or ministerial heightening or crystallization of the baptismal gift of the Spirit." (122)

Apostolicity and Apostolic Succession

In response to his critics and especially to Grelot, Schillebeeckx includes a brief section near the end of this second part on apostolicity. The issue is a crucial one given the centrality of apostolic succession to the Catholic understanding of ministry. There are, he affirms, four dimensions of apostolicity, all of which "stand in permanent reciprocal relationship." (117) These are: (i) that the "churches are founded or built up 'on the apostles and prophets' "; (ii) the apostolic content of the tradition; (iii) the actual life of believers, "i.e. following Jesus in his message, his teaching and his actions"; (iv) "the apostolicity of the church ministries, the so-called apostolic succession." (116) If all four elements are essential, the emphasis in the NT is clearly on "the apostolic content of faith." (117) The ministry and therefore apostolic succession exist to serve the apostolicity of the whole community and especially to help it maintain the apostolic tradition and the apostolic quality of its life. To recognize the necessity of the ministry, however, is not to forget the changing and historically conditioned nature of its forms. To identify apostolicity with apostolic succession in the ministry is to fall into a form of reductionism that is not only unreflective of NT teaching but also deeply destructive of ecumenical understanding.

Instead of emphasizing the contrast between the two millennia, the new historical section offers an overview of six stages in the history of the ordained ministry. The material both suggests a more gradual process of change and underlines how at every stage it was influenced by non-theological factors both in the church and in the world. Particularly striking in relation to *Ministry* is the recognition that the beginnings of a more cultic and eucharist-oriented ministry were already clear in the fourth century. The central thesis of a shift over time from a more ecclesial and pneumatic understanding to one focused on sacred power and the eucharist stands. The real points of contrast, however, are now the ante-Nicean situation and the period inaugurated by the seventeenth century. In the former the emphasis is still on pastoral leadership in and to the church. By the latter, the minister is above all the priest, the man apart, endowed with sacred powers to offer the sacrifice of the mass. New in relation to *Ministry* is the affirmation that the highly sacralized modern view was influenced by a focusing in the French school of spirituality on the divinity rather than on the humanity of Christ as the key to his priesthood.

In the course of the historical overview a number of points of detail are corrected and the much criticized section on the possibility of lay people presiding at the eucharist is dropped. New material is added, for example, on the impact of the hierarchical worldview of the Pseudo-Dionysius and on the importance of Christianity's becoming a state religion under Theodosius. The additions throughout the historical section strengthen Schillebeeckx's point that church office is an historical reality that has taken on different forms in the course of time and that these have been influenced by social, cultural, and other factors.

Part Four brings together, under the title "Listening to the 'Complaints of the People,' " some new material with material from *Ministry*. Just as any adequate theology of ministry has to recall the twists and turns of its historical course, so must it be open to contemporary negative experiences in its regard. Such "experiences of contrast" are "symptoms from which it is evident that in terms of ministry in the church the present church order at some points does more to hinder than to help the building up of the church in the gospel." (211) The section deals, at varying lengths,

with discontent among bishops, women, married priests, and critical communities. The major new material here deals with women.
The overall conclusion for the section remains unchanged: these
complaints as well as the alternative practices that have sprung up
"serve to diagnose symptoms of sickness in the existing system,
and in addition function as a criticism of the ideology which is
bound up with traditional practices." (257)

The final section is basically new. It contains a brief analysis of
two documents, the statement of the World Council of Churches on
the ministry contained in its Lima document, and the CDF's
Sacerdotium ministeriale. While recognizing in the Lima statement
"*a* (not the) legitimate and ecclesially responsible starting point for a
conversation among the churches with a view to an official consensus," (260) Schillebeeckx criticizes it for being too theoretical. It
fails to consider the fact of contemporary experience and in particular the experience of grass roots and critical communities. The
CDF's document on the other hand is judged as putting excessive, if
not exclusive, emphasis on apostolic succession in its understanding
of apostolicity. He argues here as earlier that "the apostolic content
of the Christian church" involves four essential dimensions all of
which have to be seen in their interdependence. He rejects the
suggestion that at the heart of the contemporary debate is a simple
division between a functional and an ontological understanding of
office. Like Grelot he prefers to apply ontological language to the
effects of baptism and to speak of what flows from the sacrament of
orders in functional or ministerial terms. The "functional," however, is not simply functional. The recipient of orders is related in a
sacramental way to Christ, prophet, pastor, and priest. He rejects as
inspired by the devil the "contrast between a pneuma-christological
and a direct-christological basis of both community and ministry."
They are "complementary aspects of one and the same reality."
(264)

In a brief concluding section Schillebeeckx addresses the possibility of instituting a fourth ministry alongside those of the
episcopate, presbyterate and diaconate. This would be for present
full-time pastoral workers. What the content of this office would
embrace and how it would differ from the presbyterate is not
clear. Given the considerable biblical and historical material in

the book, it is obvious that its purpose is not exhausted in this concluding suggestion. Schillebeeckx began with a pastoral problem, the contemporary shortage of priests, and with the various ways in which the contemporary church is trying to meet it. Some of the more official efforts such as Sunday services without a priest, he finds inadequate. Others, such as the alternative practices of certain small communities, are clearly outside of present canonical procedures. In *Human Face* Schillebeeckx does not seek to justify these practices but to give expression to what he believes are the authentic insights and challenges that they contain. The biblical and historical analysis is meant to relativize a certain modern understanding of the priesthood and to suggest that there is a great deal more room for flexibility than many think. The fundamental pastoral insight for Schillebeeckx is that communities need leaders and that their leadership must include the possibility of presiding at the eucharist.

Reactions to *Human Face*

According to Walter Kasper, *Human Face* maintains the fundamental thesis of *Ministry* but argues it in a more convincing and nuanced way.[13] Schillebeeckx really has shown both the relationship between office and community and the crucial importance of recognizing the historically conditioned nature of the ministry's various forms. He finds the biblical and historical material largely convincing. He also agrees with the need to deal theologically with the ongoing crisis of office with which Schillebeeckx begins.

While sympathetic to much of what Schillebeeckx says, Kasper still has a number of questions especially in relation to the treatment of the apostles. Because Schillebeeckx does not do justice to the NT emphasis on the direct relationship between the risen Christ and the apostles, he fails to appreciate the continuity between them and the idea of apostolic succession as it begins to emerge in the pastorals. Another issue for Kasper is that of the relation between the ordained ministry and the priesthood of the faithful. He finds inadequate the suggestion that the former is a crystallization of the gifts given by the baptism of the Spirit. Such a view does not do justice to the affirmation of *LG* 10 that they differ "in essence and not just in degree."

More theologically, Kasper believes that a really adequate synthesis of the pneumatological and christological aspects of ministry will only come from a renewed theology of the Trinity. What is at stake here is not only unity and difference within God and God's relationship to the world, but also the relation between Christian identity and Christian freedom, both of which office is meant to serve. For Kasper the contemporary crisis of the ordained ministry is more a spiritual crisis than a doctrinal one. The need is for a convincing spirituality of office rooted in pastoral responsibilities. He believes that Vatican II's contribution in this area has not been exhausted.

Congar singles out Schillebeeckx's more nuanced handling of apostolicity.[14] Although continuing to insist on apostolicity of faith and of practice, he now clearly recognizes the importance of "apostolic succession" in the narrow sense. His present position, in Congar's judgment, truly incorporates the different elements. Cardinal Ratzinger is less sanguine. In a letter dated September 15, 1986, the prefect of the CDF notes "that the author continues to conceive and present the apostolicity of the church in such a way that the apostolic succession through sacramental ordination represents a non-essential element for the exercise of the ministry and thus for the bestowal of the power to consecrate the eucharist— and this in opposition to the doctrine of the church."[15]

In an epilogue to the 1987 French translation of *Human Face* Schillebeeckx rejects this charge of Ratzinger and lays out in a somewhat clearer way his position on the possibility of an extraordinary minister of the eucharist.[16] His intention was not to embrace a Free Church ecclesiology or to defend the idea that anyone could preside at the eucharist. The issue is the possibility of an exceptional minister for exceptional circumstances. The basis for arguing to this possibility is the pneumatic, prophetic, and apostolic nature of the community as a whole. It provides the ontological ground for all ministry, both of the ordained and in exceptional circumstances of an extraordinary minister. He argues that the discussions at Fourth Lateran and at Trent about the need for an ordained bishop or priest to celebrate the eucharist did not include the possibility of an extraordinary minister and that therefore in their definitions such a possibility was not eliminated. The claim by Cardinal Ratzinger that the CDF's 1983 letter *Sacerdotium ministeriale* clarified the issue once and for all raises for Schillebeeckx the question of the doctrinal significance of documents issued by Roman congregations. This, he suggests, requires further investigation by theologians.

8
Ministry and Ministries:
B. Cooke

The ordained ministry has been a focus of concern for the North American (NA) Catholic Church throughout much of the post-conciliar period. Already in the late 1960s there was talk of an identity crisis among priests. The exodus of many from the active ministry as well as a drop in vocations resulted in a smaller and aging group of clergy. The initial focus of attention, especially in popular publications, was on celibacy and authority. People stressed the humanity of the priest and the need for church leaders to deal with it realistically. Related to this were arguments about the rights of priests whether to marry or to be treated as adult professionals by their bishops and superiors.

Partly in response to Vatican II's emphasis on the *presbyterium*, there was a heightened sense among priests of belonging to a community or group the members of which need to associate in various ways in order to deal with personal issues and to foster pastoral effectiveness. To some degree these groups became instruments in transforming the authoritarian relationships that sometimes existed between priests and their bishops. Diocesan and national associations dealt with such themes as the professionalization of the clergy and the implementation of the council's ecclesiology.

A particular source of concern for some priests was Vatican II's emphasis on the role of the church in the world. The optimism of the Constitution on the Church in the Modern World and

its challenge to believers to become involved in efforts to create a
more humane society raised questions for those trained in the
pre-conciliar church. The new emphasis seemed at odds with the
theology and spirituality that marked NA seminaries into the
1960s. Traditional spirituality had been almost monastic and the
lifestyle highly clerical. The new openness to the world, reinforced in the U.S. by the widespread popularity of various theologies of secularization, seemed to call for a different vision of
the priest as well as for a more worldly spirituality. Not surprisingly, many priests became dissatisfied with what was called a
"cultic" model of the priesthood. Some wanted priests to be
prophets, while others sought a solution in the "hyphenated
priest," the priest-psychologist or priest-social worker.

It is no exaggeration to say that for many in the late 1960s and
early 1970s the religious ideal of the priesthood that they had been
given in the seminary collapsed. It had been a highly spiritual one,
rooted in the religious traditions of seventeenth century France, in
the traditions of Bérulle, Jean Eudes, Vincent de Paul, and the
Sulpicians. In some cases the collapse was accompanied by a with-
drawal from the priesthood; in other cases priests were motivated
to seek a new theology and a new spirituality.

A Problem of Language

Over the last twenty-five years there has continued to be a
considerable confusion and difference of opinion about the meaning and centrality of the language of priest and priesthood. The
sacerdotal understanding of the presbyterate had been central, as
already indicated, both at Trent and in the spirituality that was
dominant up to the council. The realization that the language of
priesthood was not used for the ministry in the NT has provoked
three different kinds of response. On the basis of its absence from
the NT, some have argued that it is a foreign import from pagan or
OT sources and that it ought to be eliminated. Others have taken
the opposite tack. For them the fact that it came to be used in the
course of the first centuries is justification enough for its continued
use today. Still others, while open to the developments that took
place, believe that the practice of the NT at least signals that there

are dangers here which if disregarded could lead to an obscuring of fundamental gospel truths.

The language of priesthood has also been central to another area of debate. One of the most striking features of Vatican II's reception in NA was the enthusiasm with which its teaching on the laity was greeted. If there were differences about the relative importance of their role in the world and in the church, there was widespread agreement that the council's emphasis on them was one of the most positive developments of recent church history. Lay involvement became a key factor in liturgical renewal. Lay persons began to act as readers and as ministers of communion. Perhaps most important was the sense that the eucharist was not just the mass of the priest, but a celebration of all believers who in virtue of their baptismal priesthood are enabled to take an active part in it. The more widespread the language of the priesthood of the faithful became, the more people began to raise questions about the distinctiveness of the priesthood of the ordained. There has probably been no text of Vatican II on the ordained ministry cited more frequently than LG 10 and especially its affirmation that the "common priesthood of the faithful and the ministerial or hierarchical priesthood . . . differ essentially and not only in degree." For some the text is self-evident, needing only to be quoted to resolve any difficulty. For others it is more controversial and requires a nuanced exegesis.

Ministry and Ministries

If the language of priesthood was and, to some extent, continues to be a focus of the debate about the relation between the laity and the ordained, it has, especially in NA, tended increasingly to be overshadowed by the language of "ministry." For a number of reasons and to a degree unknown in Europe, "ministry" became by the early 1970s the key term not only for the ordained but also for what Vatican II, using an older terminology, still called "the apostolate of the laity."

In some cases "ministry" became so broad in its meaning that it seemed to be all but interchangeable with Christian life itself. In virtue of baptism and the various gifts of the Spirit that baptism

entails, everyone is called to some form of ministry, whether full-
or part-time, spontaneous or structured, presupposing a professional preparation or based simply on gifts of nature and grace. As
seminaries and faculties of theology found more lay people and
religious women among their students, they began to describe their
programs as preparing people not for priesthood but for ministry.
The vagueness of the term soon led to disappointments. One and
the same program could not prepare people for all the various
forms of ministry in which they were interested. Some specifica-
tions had to be introduced, and some distinctions made.

The phenomenon of team ministry involving professionally
trained lay people as well as priests has been another factor in
raising the question about the distinctive nature of the ordained
priesthood. Is it focused on the sacramental, especially the eucharist and reconciliation, or is its task more a form of leadership,
including the calling out and coordinating of other ministries? Perhaps more fundamental is the question whether the ordained priesthood can be treated in isolation at all or whether it can only be
understood alongside, and in relation to, other forms of ministry.

The use of the language of ministry in place of that of office
and priesthood has inevitably led many to think of the ordained as
having a function rather than as constituting a class or having a
particular status. Ministry suggests something to be done, a task to
be fulfilled, a need to be met. When this approach is combined
with an historical awareness of the changes that the priesthood has
undergone over the centuries, it leads to a sense of flexibility. A
new cultural situation, new evangelical challenges, new needs
within the community: such things cry out for generosity and cre-
ativity in developing forms of ministry that will be adequate to
them. Such an emphasis is more easily open to the ordination of
married as well as single persons, and of women as well as men.

As indicated in earlier chapters, the language of ministry is
rooted in the NT use of *diakonia,* service. For many writers over
the last decades the notion of service represents a necessary correc-
tive to clerical and hierarchical emphases. Ministry exists in and
for the service of the community. It is not self-justifying but has to
prove itself pragmatically. The theme of service suggests a profound religious attitude of identity with the self-giving love of

Christ, who came not to be served but to serve. In a church redis-covering the active participation to which the laity are called, it points to an understanding of leadership that is collaborative and empowering.

It is striking to note how little of the theological writing in NA over the last twenty-five years has dealt with the ordained ministry in religious congregations. The model of the presbyterate at Vati-can II, as much as the council expressly includes religious priests, is focused on the diocesan clergy and more specifically on the pastor. The centrality given to the bishop with his pastoral, prophetic and priestly functions points in the same direction. Many, though by no means all, who have written recently on the ordained ministry have insisted on the pastoral as the focal point in relation to which the sacramental and preaching functions are to be seen. The con-text for the ministry tends to be the stable, local community in which the presbyters exercise their responsibility in close collabora-tion with the diocesan bishop.

Such emphases raise questions about the practice of religious priests, past and present. A number of authors have touched on this in passing. Donald Senior, for example, relates the double structure of charismatic and institutional ministries in the NT to religious and secular priests.[1] The Jesuit historian John O'Malley has addressed the issue, to my knowledge, more consistently than anyone else. In a 1988 article in *Theological Studies* he argues that Vatican II's vision is too narrow and that it needs to be comple-mented by a better knowledge of the way in which the ministry has in fact been carried out over the centuries. He contrasts the "church type" approach of the secular clergy to the more "sect type" experience of many of the orders. It is this latter that needs to be retrieved and integrated into our thinking about the ordained ministry if we are not to be enormously impoverished.[2]

Some of the most forward looking reflection in NA on priest-hood and ministry has been provoked by ecumenical concerns. Among the many national and international discussions with Angli-can, Orthodox, and other Christian Churches that have dealt ex-plicitly with the theme, the U.S. Lutheran/Roman Catholic dia-logue holds a unique place. Unlike the patristic emphasis of some dialogues, it has focused attention both on the critique of the reformation and on the uniquely normative character of the NT. The desire by Catholic scholars to recognize in some way the validity of the Lutheran ministry has led to a rethinking of the notion of "validity" as well as of the meaning and import of apostolic succession. Some have appealed to NT pluralism to argue for the possibility of a variety of church orders, non-episcopal as well as episcopal.

The ecumenical dialogues have emphasized what in fact has been a truism within recent Roman Catholic theology, namely the necessity of history as a presupposition for any adequate theology of ministry. Like the church, the ordained ministry is an historical reality that has lived within, and interacted with, a variety of political, cultural and social contexts. There is a history both of its practice and of the theology that has developed in relation to it that needs to be taken into account in present rethinking. Among recent historical surveys published in the U.S., one of the more balanced and accessible is Kenan Osborne's *Priesthood: A History of the Ordained Ministry in the Roman Catholic Church*.[3] In spite of its title, it focuses more on theology and on official church documents than on practice, although it does make clear how, in a general sense, practice influences theory.

The book offers an historical context for understanding Vatican II's theology of the ordained ministry. The conciliar positions seem to guide the choice of topics and to influence the relative emphasis given to them. It recounts in some detail, for example, the growth in the early church of the role of the episcopate with its increasing pastoral and liturgical responsibilities. The increased importance of the presbyterate in the medieval west is shown to be related to a number of societal and ecclesial developments. The decrees of the Council of Trent are exposed at some length. These offer both a background and a context for the work of Vatican II. Its contribution is described as an overcoming of the narrowness of the modern tradition. While not rejecting the teaching of Trent, the council balances it with its rediscovery of the episcopal and pastoral emphases of the early church.

Osborne's own theology is markedly christocentric. Jesus is the model and pattern of all ministry. People are called to it, not by the church, but by the risen Lord. Although Osborne affirms an ecclesiological dimension to ministry, the emphasis, as with Ratzinger, Galot and John Paul II, is consistently on Christ. There is at the same time very little mention of the role of the Spirit. As positive as he is about Vatican II, Osborne underlines the unfinished character of its teaching. Questions remain about such things as the precise nature of the priestly office of Jesus, about collegiality, about the relation between ordained and unordained ministry, and about the nature of ordination itself.

Women and the Priesthood

Since the early 1970s there has been a great deal of writing, pro and con, about the ordination of women. In addition to arguments in favor of women's ordination, feminist theologians have challenged the traditional understanding of the ministry. Sometimes this is formulated in general terms as a rejection of clericalism and "hierarchicalism," both of which are seen as manifestations of patriarchalism and sexism. It is sometimes argued that the earliest levels of the NT reveal a more egalitarian and charismatic sense of ministry than had previously been thought. Like so many others during the same period, some feminist writers have made a great deal of the NT use of *diakonia.* This is interpreted as undermining all forms of domination and authoritarianism. While recognizing the positive intentions behind recent efforts to develop a "servant ecclesiology," Elizabeth Schüssler Fiorenza rejects such a theology for its failure to "seriously challenge the church's structure of patriarchal hierarchy and the 'class' division between the ordained and non-ordained ministers."[4] Far from abolishing "the clerical 'class' division between clergy and laity," the language of ordained ministry as "servant leadership . . . mystifies and perpetuates it."[5]

Various writings of Rosemary Ruether suggest a radical theology of ministry. "The present clerical and institutional structure" is opposed to the gospel and needs to be transformed. Her emphasis is communitarian. "Any Christian community gathering together with the intention of being the Church of Christ has the power to celebrate the Lord's Supper as an expression of their common life."[6] The idea that "priests possess sacramental 'powers' which the community does not have" is false and needs to be demystified.[7]

Recent writings on the ministry reflect different and sometimes opposing concerns and are guided by quite distinctive methodologies. Feminist, ecumenical, liturgical, and liberationist perspectives inevitably highlight both critically and positively different aspects of the one reality. Another way of distinguishing the various approaches is to note the criteria to which they appeal. Some focus on the contemporary church and on the challenges and needs with which it is currently struggling. Sociological and cultural analysis looms large in this approach, and if there is an appeal to history it is primarily to free the church from the narrowness of the recent tradition. Other approaches tend to be more explicitly theological. Here people differ in the relative weight they give to, and the way they interpret, Vatican II, Trent, the patristic model, and the NT itself. While recognizing the uniquely normative character of the NT, some read it through the eyes of later periods while others seek in it, and especially in its early phases, a critical norm against which subsequent developments can be measured.

Concern for Identity

Debates about the theology of the ordained ministry have been judged by some to be a significant factor in the identity crisis of many priests. In response some recent books and articles have called for greater clarity and above all a clearer and more forceful expression of the uniqueness of the priestly office. The emphases of John Paul II and of theologians like Ratzinger and Galot have found a considerable echo. Cardinal William Baum, in a 1988 address on the results of the Vatican-sponsored visitation of American seminaries, affirms that the major issue that surfaced in the course of it was the question about the nature of the priesthood. "The seminaries in the US that are the most successful are those that hand on to their students a clear idea of the priesthood thoroughly grounded in theology and in whole hearted fidelity to the Magisterium."[8]

The cardinal lists four inner church factors that make it difficult today for seminaries to fulfill their responsibilities in this area. These are: "the rather generalized concept of ministry," the widespread notion of the priesthood of the faithful, the debates about celibacy, and the discussion touching on the ordination of women. For Cardinal Baum, the ordained ministry is rooted in that of the twelve. Although the precise form of it developed slowly, "the central fact of an ordained, hierarchical ministry is plain; and it emerged as tri-partite: bishops, priest and deacons."[9] To stress what a priest does is inadequate. As the traditional doctrine of the "character" makes clear, ordination modifies a person's being.

The rest of the present and the whole of the following chapter will offer a brief overview of what some individual NA theologians have written about priesthood and ministry. The treatment is by no means exhaustive, either in terms of the individuals cited or in relation to all those who have written on the topic. All that can be said is that these authors have made substantial contributions that continue to be a part of the ongoing discussion.

Bernard Cooke

One of the most substantial works on the theme of priesthood and ministry in the post-conciliar period is Bernard Cooke's 1976 *Ministry to Word and Sacrament.*[10] What is perhaps most distinctive about it is the breadth of its treatment of history. Much more inclusive in the forms of ministry it investigates than Osborne's survey of the ordained ministry, it has rightly been called encyclopedic in the range of the issues it broaches.

For Cooke ministry is an historical reality, very much influenced in its forms by particular cultures and changing ecclesial needs. His interest is not to show how developments leading to medieval, Tridentine or even Vatican II understandings took place, but rather to stress the historically conditioned character of all ministry. In doing so he hopes to free the contemporary church to meet the needs of the present day. History in this regard needs to be complemented by present discernment.

The book is divided into five parts each of which evokes an essential element of what Christian ministry involves or at least has involved. Rejecting as inadequate Vatican II's threefold model of pastor, prophet, and priest, Cooke organizes his presentation under the following headings: formation of community, word, service, God's judgment, and the church's sacramentality. The parts are subdivided into chapters the last of which in each case presents Cooke's own theological synthesis. The others deal with successive periods in church history.

Although space prevents any extended treatment of the historical material, a number of themes should at least be mentioned as they are echoed in much recent writing. Cooke gives a special place to the NT and above all to the practice of Jesus. Although the historical Jesus is referred to as *the* criterion for ministry and priesthood, equal and finally greater weight is given to the risen Christ and to the Spirit. Ministry exists in the church. As much as it took its origin in the life and saving activity of Jesus, it is more immediately the place where the risen Christ continues to act through his Spirit. Divine law (*ius divinum*) has to be understood not in terms of an historical institution by Jesus but rather in relation to an ongoing and faith-filled response of the church to the impulse of the risen Christ.

In spite of his stress on the continuing activity of Christ, Cooke has a clear preference for the NT over later developments. In a general sense he sees the early decades of Christianity as marked by pluralism and by an emphasis on charisms. The historical process is from charism to institution and from variety to uniformity. He particularly regrets the tendency of the episcopacy to appropriate all the different ministries to itself. If the early church knew independent prophets, teachers and traveling apostles, the patristic period witnessed the triumph of an episcopal structure. All ministry now belongs to the bishops who allow presbyters and deacons to share in it to a certain degree. A more organic model of church has been replaced by a monarchical one. The Spirit is more and more subject to the control of the institution.

A Distortion of the Gospel

The pattern of a primitive ideal that is more or less lost in the course of history is repeated in several of the sections. It is particularly evident in the treatment of the priestly interpretation of the ministry. Like so many others, Cooke points out that in the NT priestly language is used of Christ and of the whole community but not of community leaders. From the beginning Christianity had its own distinctive ritual actions in baptism and the eucharist, but the emphasis in both cases remained on the word. Inseparable from evangelization and proclamation, both are inherently prophetic. In this sense even the liturgical leader is primarily a prophetic figure, "one who publicly voices the blessing, the witness to God's saving action in Christ, the prophet whose own word carries the divine word of power and authority." (530)

What happened historically was that the prophetic understanding of liturgical leaders gradually gave way to a priestly one. Bishops and presbyters were increasingly seen as "cult personnel." A major factor in this "cultifying of Christianity" (541) was the growing influence of the OT. Cooke's judgment of the process is reminiscent of that of the great Lutheran historian Adolf von Harnack. There seems to be a theory of decadence at work. Early Christianity rapidly lost sight of "the radical newness of the Gospels" (542) and fell back into OT ways of thinking.

For Cooke the shift from ministry to priesthood is a shift from function to a state of being. It marks the inevitable beginning of the practice of viewing the ordained as a "sacred group," "set apart" from the community at large and enjoying a level of existence that lifts them above the laity. What was thus begun so early was intensified with the passing centuries. Augustine's notion of cosmic order and the Pseudo-Dionysius' speculations on the heavenly hierarchy reinforced and gave a metaphysical justification to the ecclesio-sociological reality of the clergy/laity split. This split represents for Cooke a serious "deviation from the authentic ideal of a Christian community." (197) It is something that must be overcome if the church is going to be able to respond creatively to present needs.

Cooke is most negative in his treatment of ministry to God's judgment. Once again he sees a more community-based, Spirit inspired, prophetically mediated form of judgment giving way to a judgment process almost entirely in the hands of bishops. Cyprian is said to be "largely responsible for crystallizing a 'political' understanding of the episcopal office." With Cyprian himself, however, the bishop is still a charismatic figure. As bishops are more influenced by civil models and become dominated by canonical norms, judgment becomes totally institutionalized. It is a central conviction of Cooke in this section and elsewhere that whether the issue is teaching or the discernment and condemnation of sin, office as such has no special rights. What is needed is competency and/or the prophetic gift. Central to judgment in a Christian context is conscience and its convictions and insights and over against it the prophetic challenge. Here again the prophetic turns out to be at the heart of Christian ministry.

For Cooke, jurisdiction in the technical sense of having to do with law and external behavior has no place in the church. He rejects the juridical interpretation of the priest's role in penance as well as "the idea that authority to teach [is] derived from office." (519) The medieval distinction between orders and jurisdiction is no longer helpful and should be abandoned. Although some kind of certification for preachers is required, "this does not mean that preaching as such is linked with office or with any kind of jurisdictional authority." (332)

Ministry as Sacrament

The most extensive and most positive treatment of the presbyterate comes in the section dealing with ministry to the church's sacramentality. Jesus is the criterion for any possible meaning of priesthood within a Christian context. In his case priesthood involved a whole life of love and service, a life in which all believers share in virtue of baptism. "It is the Christian community that is priestly/sacramental in its whole being." (644) The priesthood of liturgical celebrants has to be understood in relation to the priestly character of the community. "It flows from the more basic priesthood of the community, functions for the sake of that community priesthood, and in a sense is a specialized or intensified expression of that common priesthood." (641) In the liturgy the celebrant represents the community but also, and in a special way, Christ. Where others have attempted to explain this relationship to Christ by speaking of the celebrant as the vicar or legate of Christ, as someone who acts *in persona Christi,* Cooke describes his function as "sacramental in the strict sense," i.e. as symbolizing and rendering present what it symbolizes.

Traditional and especially popular notions have tended to think of Christ as distant and yet somehow brought close by the sacramental activity of the ordained priest. For Cooke, Christ is already present in the community and in the world. What the ordained minister does is make his presence sacramentally visible. In his liturgical functions he is the sacrament of Christ. It is in this sense that Cooke understands the traditional notion of ordination as a sacrament. Through ordination one enters and becomes a part of a *collegium* responsible for liturgical leadership and for witness to the apostolic faith. Word and sacrament are central to presbyteral responsibility. Theoretically these two elements could be separated from governing and other leadership functions. In fact, however, from earliest times they have been joined. Cooke insists, however, that leadership involves other people besides the ordained.

Overall Cooke stresses the need to broaden one's starting point for thinking about priesthood and ministry. How they are understood will depend enormously on one's ecclesiology and soteriology. Cooke himself emphasizes the present activity of the risen Christ and the Spirit in the world as well as in the church. It is an emphasis that has implications for the meaning of human life in history. It implies a certain desacralization.

In order to renew the ministry we will have to move beyond present forms. In spite of positive things about bishops and the laity, Vatican II "provides little guidance for theological exploration into the nature of ministry or for creative expansion of ministry in response to contemporary needs." (7) The study of history indicates how one-sided and historically conditioned the traditional Roman Catholic understanding of priesthood is. The model of a clerical group, endowed through ordination with sacred power and placed over against a basically passive laity, fails to do justice to the NT and offers no hope for the renewal that the contemporary situation of the church and the world demands.

The emphasis should be on the community and on the fact that all believers are called to an active sharing in its life and mission. All receive gifts of the Spirit, all in one way or another are called to ministry. The pastoral leadership of bishops and presbyters is essential, but it should be focused on fostering and coordinating the gifts and talents of others. To do this they themselves must rediscover their charismatic roots. They need to be desacralized and freed from legalistic and institutional modes of thinking and acting.

The emphasis is not on particular offices and structures but on the community and its needs. Certain things have to be done, various roles and functions have to be accepted, if the church is to fulfill its mission. What is required is not just ministry but ministries, ministries that issue from the very nature of the community and the present prompting of the Spirit. The ordained ministry must operate not in isolation but in collaboration with a whole range of other ministries.

9

Tavard, O'Meara, Kilmartin and Dulles

Among the large number of theologians in North America who have written recently on the theme of the ordained ministry, the present chapter will focus on only four, the first of whom is George Tavard. A well-known systematic theologian with extensive experience in ecumenical dialogue, he published in 1983 a revised version of earlier articles under the title *A Theology for Ministry*.[1] While sharing certain concerns and positions with Cooke's study, it represents on a number of points a relatively distinctive perspective. It is clearly sensitive, for example, not only to the issues arising out of the reformation, but also to the experience of eastern Christianity. It is perhaps because of influence from it that he insists on the need for a trinitarian approach.

Tavard situates the ordained ministry within a broader sense of ministry and mission and these in turn within an understanding of Catholicism. He begins not with the historical Jesus or with the experience of the first decades of Christianity but with the massive historical fact of Catholicism. Although his experience is primarily with its western form, what he says about Catholicity has a wider application than Roman Catholicism.

Catholicity has to do with wholeness. It involves the whole of God's creative and redemptive plan at the center of which is the fact of the incarnation of the Word and the actualization in time of its implications through the activity of the Spirit. Given the

119

incarnation, it is no surprise that Catholicism should put such an emphasis on the sacraments which it sees as "privileged moments" for facilitating that communion with God which is at the heart of the Catholic vision. The centrality of the sacraments underlines and presupposes the communal or social dimension of the church.

If Catholicism is the basis for Tavard's reflections about ministry, the eucharist provides the more immediate horizon within which his theology is worked out. The church is above all a eucharistic fellowship rooted in and sustained by its continuing celebration of the eucharistic body of Christ. Church and eucharist belong together. There is a dynamic sequence and ongoing mutual interrelationship among four factors: the incarnation, the eucharist, the community, and its missionary service. "The church is grounded in Christ, nurtured by the eucharistic presence, built up as a community, and it sends its members on their mission in the world for the kingdom." (51) In this fourfold sequence, Tavard recognizes what he calls the fourfold responsibility of ministers: "proclamation, liturgy, education, and service."

Like Cooke, Tavard finds the threefold division of the ministry adopted by Vatican II to be somewhat arbitrary. It results from "a considerable oversimplification of the tasks of Christ as described in the Scriptures. Jesus is not only priest, prophet, and king; he is also Son of man, lamb of God, servant of Yahweh, friend, shepherd, healer, fire-bringer, preacher, rabbi." (127) The scope of the ministry becomes even more truncated when the threefold office as applied to the ordained is reduced to "sanctification, teaching, and government."

Structures of Ministry

Tavard believes that what he calls the "structures of ministry" can be discerned either by looking at the history of the church or by reflecting theologically on its nature and present situation. The church exists between the first and second comings of Christ. Rooted in the first, it looks forward to, and is drawn toward, eschatological fulfillment in Christ's final advent. The four structures correspond to four central aspects of the work of Christ. He is the mediator, the prophet of the good news who both preaches the word and sends the Spirit, the servant, and the divine pedagogue or teacher.

Different traditions have tended to emphasize one or other of the structures to the detriment of the others. What needs to be recognized is that all four belong to the essence of ministry. Without mediation, proclamation, service and education, the church would not be what Christ intended it to be. To recognize this, however, is not to say anything about the form the different structures should take and whether, for example, they all are equally central to an understanding of the ordained.

There is a sense in which everyone is called to make some contribution to all aspects of ministry. Here is the meaning of the notion of "a general or universal priesthood of all believers." Such a broad sense of ministry, however, does not preclude the need for an ordained ministry. Although it could be involved in all four aspects, its special domain is the liturgy and proclamation. The existence of such a specialized ministry, "connected with the structures of mediation and of proclamation, is rooted in the NT pattern of apostleship." (86)

Although he regards ordination as a sacrament, Tavard does not believe that ordination by a bishop is an absolutely necessary condition for liturgical ministry. "The essential is that a certain person be recognized by the church as one of its ministers." (86) His position here seems to be influenced by his general judgment about the episcopacy. In spite of Vatican II's position on the topic, he maintains that there are two possible historical interpretations for the relationship between bishops and presbyters: one can think of the monarchic episcopacy as rising out of the presbyterate or of the presbyterate descending from the episcopacy. He opts for the former. "History favors the fundamental identity of priesthood and episcopacy, rather than the theory of an intrinsic difference between them." (119)

Priestly Ministry

Tavard's approach to the priestly interpretation of the ministry is, to my knowledge, unique. He recognizes the absence of priestly language for the ministry within the NT. The use of it for Christ and the community in Hebrews, 1 Peter, and Revelation is interpreted eschatologically. The NT priesthood is "a celestial model" for the church. It was only because of "the trauma of the indefinite delay of the parousia" (120) that it was brought down to earth and embodied in the ministry of bishops and presbyters. The development was in no sense a deviation from the gospel or a fall back into OT categories. It was "a theological necessity. The alternative was not a functional ministry rather than a cultic priesthood; it was despair of the eschatological kingdom." (121) It is the eschatological nature of the church with its inner longing for fulfillment in the heavenly temple that demands that there should be a priesthood in it. "Its identification with the ministry of wisdom [presbyterate] and administration [episcopate] was perhaps not necessary, but it was hardly avoidable."

The origin of the ministry as it now exists is clearly complex. It derives from the coming together in a single set of office-holders of the pastoral oversight of the church with the eschatological priesthood. Thus Catholic priests and bishops "do not descend directly from the apostles. . . . They succeed the second century bishops and priests, who besides their functions of pastoral care, preaching and oversight, accepted also the task of mediating, for their concrete historical community, the eschatological *hierateuma* or *sacerdotium* of the heavenly People of God." (121)

This positive interpretation of the introduction of priestly terminology frees Tavard from "the fear of a 'cultic priesthood' " (93 n1) which he sees operative in the work of Schillebeeckx, Küng, and others who insist on the primacy of pastoral leadership. Interestingly, Tavard relates the ministry of education to Christ's pastoral and not to his prophetic office. As for the traditional notion of governing, he finds it largely irrelevant to Christian ministry. What is positive in the idea comes to a large degree under the ministry of the word. Like Cooke, Tavard has little time for a juridical approach to church leadership. "Discipline as discipline we should cheerfully abandon; discipline as developing receptivity to the gospel, unanimity in the body of Christ, obedience to the Spirit, we must cling fast to." (136)

Priesthood and Eucharist

Both history and theology reveal the centrality of the eucharist to the ministerial priesthood. "The priesthood is centered on the eucharist, not only as the 'apex', but first of all as the 'fount' of all its functions. Structurally, it is the foundation as well as the keystone of the ministry." (131) Ordination is significant because by it one is "set apart" in order to preside at the eucharist. The traditional notion of the "character" can be thought of as "the orientation of the priest toward the eucharist." (132) Tavard concludes his book by reiterating sixteen suggestions that he had made in 1968 for reorganizing the ministry. The opening statement could hardly be more clear. "The work of the priest should be centered exclusively on sacramental activity; his main task is to lead the eucharistic prayer and to preside over the sacramental life of the faithful." (157) Given that sacrament and word are inseparable this has to be understood to include the ministry of the word. But the cultic and eucharistic focus is unmistakable.

As much as Tavard insists on the necessary and privileged relation of priesthood and eucharist, he is not simply reiterating the position of Trent. Clearly wanting to go beyond the somewhat simplistic traditional approach to the eucharist as sacrament and sacrifice, he suggests that the role of the presiding minister involves four main points. In the first place the minister acts as a kind of mystagogue, initiating people ever more profoundly into the mystery of Christ. Although a representative of the people, the priest also acts "in the person of Christ," bringing his mystery to the community and helping its members to enter into it. This calls for and makes sense of "an ontological link between the minister and Christ's own priesthood by way of ordination." (194) Such a link frees the community from the minister's subjectivity and guarantees that it is indeed the Lord to whom they relate.

The minister also acts as a "hierarch," as someone who testifies to and embodies the action of Jesus at the last supper. Such a person is of necessity a teacher and minister of the word. This applies not only to the homily but to the whole of the eucharistic celebration at the heart of which is the proclamation of Christ's death and resurrection. The meal aspect of the eucharist uncovers the final aspect of the minister's role in it. To preside at the meal is also to serve the needs of the congregation. With traditional Catholic theology, Tavard speaks of the sacrificial role of the priest. He insists, however, that this is inseparable from the activity of the whole community. In the eucharistic prayer "the priest acts as instrument of the church associating itself with Christ's sacrifice, and as instrument of Christ presenting himself before the Father." (113)

Distinctive of Tavard's approach is his differentiation between the ordained minister as elder and as priest. As elder the minister is the trusted representative of the community and as such "should be esthetically acceptable to them." (100) As priest the minister is "the recipient of a special sacrament or ordination from which a new function derives. This is not delegated by the people but one has been called to it by God." (101) Catholic theology, he argues, has given little thought to the minister as elder, although it has stressed his priestly character. The Protestant tradition has done the opposite.

For all Tavard's emphasis on the priestly nature of the ordained minister and for all his focusing on the eucharist, it is clear that his position is not without its challenges to present practice. His unwillingness, in particular, to identify the priesthood with pastoral leadership opens up the possibility if not the necessity of a new approach. The emphasis is on tasks that need to be performed if the church is to fulfill its mission. He envisages these as the responsibility not of a single person but of a team. All ministries should be open to women as well as to men, and to the married as well as to celibates. As long as the fourfold structure of ministry is respected, Tavard favors a considerable flexibility in regard to form.

Thomas O'Meara

Like Cooke, Tavard, and other NA theologians, O'Meara approaches the issue of the priesthood or, in his terms, of the presbyterate and the episcopacy, within a broad sense of ministry. His starting point is the contemporary church. In spite of fewer priests and religious, the present situation is not entirely negative.

He points in particular to the large number of lay people preparing themselves for, and actively involved in, forms of ministry. His 1983 book *Theology of Ministry*[2] was written in order to make sense of this development and to help give it some direction. His secondary interest is to strengthen the presbyterate and episcopate in their particular ministries.

The book offers "a fundamental theology of ministry" at the heart of which is "a theology of grace which views God's presence in the world as the source, milieu and goal of ministry." (1) Ministry is not something that was given once and for all and in fixed forms that simply has to be maintained and periodically renewed. It is a developing, changing reality, responsive to both culture and the ever new prompting of the Spirit.

The person and practice of Jesus remain normative for all thinking about ministry. The aspects of his ministry that O'Meara stresses are reflective of some of his own major concerns. Jesus both preached the kingdom of God and dedicated his life to its service. The church and its ministry are to do the same. The kingdom, while not identified with the church, is to some degree present within it, present through the Spirit and through what Catholics have traditionally called grace. Present in people, it is a dynamic reality that is meant to have an impact through them on the world at large. Although grace is anonymously present wherever people struggle to overcome evil and further what is good, it comes to sacramental visibility in the community of the church where in word and ritual it is celebrated and proclaimed and brought to bear on the life of individuals.

The emphasis on the kingdom and on the Spirit distinguishes Christianity from OT and pagan forms of religion. Without embracing the position of a Karl Barth, O'Meara stresses the opposition between faith and religion and by that fact the discontinuity between the levitical priesthood and the ministry of the NT. Christ's priesthood and by extension the priesthood of the community of faith do not continue the priesthood of Aaron but represent realities of a different order. In Jesus, life itself, life lived in faith and obedience to God and in self-giving love for others, is the sacrifice. His ministry marks a certain desacralization in the history of religion, a desacralization, however, that has nothing to do with secularization. Everything about him relates to God, but to God as present not in a separated temple with a hieratic ritual, but in the midst of life. The absence in the NT of priestly terminology for the various ministries that then existed is not by chance. It witnesses to the transformation of the idea of religion for which Christianity stands. In the light of this the gradual "sacerdotalization" of the NT ministry in subsequent centuries can only be judged in a negative light. Here and in related issues, O'Meara's position is markedly different from that of Tavard.

Historical Variations

Because the forms and the theology of ministry have changed so radically over time, it is important to have some sense of history if only to be able to free oneself to deal creatively with contemporary challenges and possibilities. O'Meara evokes six periods in each of which the ministry underwent a significant metamorphosis. He describes what took place in the earliest phase as a shift from minister to bishop. The NT knew a multiplicity of ministries rooted in a variety of charisms. The process in the second century and later was for these to be gradually taken over by the bishops who, in turn, as their communities grew, shared them out in a structured and controlled way. Here is the beginning of what in a global sense can be described as "a diminution" of ministry, a collapsing of its rich and vital diversity into a single office. This process was accompanied by a tendency to understand the episcopacy in terms of civil society. "The organization of the church brought Roman order, modest diversity, and liturgical membership where earlier there had been community, pneumatic discernment, ministerial diversity, and charismatic individuality." (104) This growing "episcopalization" of the ministry was paralleled by its progressive "sacerdotalization." (101)

What was thus begun in the patristic period underwent further modifications under the influence in the early middle ages of the monastic model and then in the thirteenth century of the triumph of hierarchical thinking in the great theological syntheses of that period. Pseudo-Dionysius and his cosmic hierarchical vision reinforced the feudal tendency to replace "the circle of different charisms" with "the pyramid of hierarchy." (111) In an insightful phrase, O'Meara describes this as an "aesthetical ecclesiology" in which "beauty and life flowed from order." (112) That this view placed the eucharist at the center of Christian life underlined the sense of the priest as the consecrated person set apart to offer the sacrifice and to distribute God's grace to a passive laity.

Equally insightful is the treatment of the two last periods, the baroque and the romantic. The first of these is dominated by the model and the influence of the Jesuits. Ministry is inseparable from the great drama of grace which is played out within the soul of the individual priest or religious. Catholic romanticism reinforced the tendency to isolate the individual priest and to emphasize his personal and, in a spiritual sense at least, his private identification with the sacrifice of Christ.

O'Meara's historical overview is less encyclopedic than that of Cooke and not as focused as that of Schillebeeckx. Its purpose is to suggest how in the course of history different aspects of the ministry have been stressed and how in the process genuine values have been lost. It also is intended to bring out the importance of culture. What is happening in the world has an enormous impact on the actual forms that ministry takes in any given period.

"Primal Ministry"

In spite of his basically non-judgmental attitude to the history of ministry, O'Meara's main source of inspiration in his effort to develop new forms to meet contemporary needs is none of the periods he describes but the NT itself. To underline the unique significance of the experience of the early church, he calls its practice "primal ministry." It reflects four characteristics that ought to be kept in mind in looking at contemporary possibilities. Church ministry initially was not a "sacred office." It represented something radically new over against the age-old phenomenon of "cultic priesthood." Not itself a state of life, ministry, as its name suggests, involves a task, an activity, something that can best be described not with nouns but with verbs. Ministry is always related to the kingdom of God. It exists in the community of the church in order to build it up and to serve it as it attempts to fulfill its mandate and mission in regard to the kingdom. Finally, ministry in the NT is "universal and diverse." It is something to which everyone is called in virtue of baptism and which therefore inevitably takes on a multiplicity of forms. Diversity, however, was never intended as an occasion for division. Diverse ministries need to be exercised in harmony.

Building on these characteristics, O'Meara offers a definition which he thinks can illuminate and direct contemporary efforts at restructuring. "Christian ministry is the public activity of a baptized follower of Jesus Christ flowing from the Spirit's charism and an individual personality on behalf of a Christian community to witness to, serve and realize the kingdom of God." (142) Although this definition clearly goes beyond the traditional threefold ministry of bishop, presbyter, and deacon, it is not so broad as to embrace all forms of Christian life. O'Meara is convinced that to call everything ministry "will ultimately hand over ministry again to a professional class." (159) Ministry involves public and explicit activity at the service of the church and the kingdom. It is not to be identified with discipleship.

Episcopate and presbyterate are to be understood primarily in terms of leadership. To be ordained to either office is to accept a responsibility of pastoral leadership involving preaching, presiding at the liturgy, directing the apostolic and liturgical life of the community, and facilitating and coordinating other ministries. The model here for O'Meara as for Schillebeeckx is the early church. As important as these traditional forms of ministry are, however, they need to be complemented by others. Particular mention is made of ministries of education, of peace and justice, and of health care. Such ministries already exist and are being filled on a full-time basis by people who have prepared themselves professionally for them.

New Forms of Ministry

The existence of such forms of lay ministry make the present situation a more positive one than might at first glance appear. To appreciate the real significance, however, of what is happening, one has to move beyond the term "lay ministry." It continues to reflect the traditional but unhelpful distinction between clergy and laity. What is needed is a recognition that what such people are doing on the basis of their sense of vocation and their training is simply a ministry and that it should be viewed as such. In the Catholic tradition recognition of comparable realities is done by ordination.

O'Meara stresses the importance of presbyters even as he rejects a sacerdotal interpretation of their office. His intent in calling for the ordination of new forms of ministry is neither to undermine the meaning of ordination nor to belittle the distinctive ordination of presbyters and bishops. Their ordination needs to be taken seriously although it should be understood more in relation to the presence of the Spirit to the whole community than simply in terms of the ordaining bishop and his sacramental power. A diversity of ministries calls for a diversity of rituals by which individuals' charisms are recognized and celebrated and by which they are commissioned and endowed with those further gifts of the Spirit without which they cannot fulfill their responsibilities.

In concluding O'Meara insists that he does not want to weaken but to strengthen the offices of priest and bishop. Theirs is a "demanding leadership" involving as it does the coordination of "a panoply of ministers—full-time and part-time." (210) Their "leading ministerial role, within similar but diverse ministries, grounds the responsibility of presiding at Eucharist and of focusing and maintaining union with the church's tradition and universality." (209)

O'Meara's insistence on leadership and action and on the need to overcome the clergy/laity split should not be interpreted as a capitulation to the process of secularization. If he reacts against the traditional emphasis on state of life over activity, he knows that doing is grounded in being, and that the activity of presbyters as indeed of all ministers is rooted both in the gift of the Spirit and in the depth and authenticity of their response to that gift. Desacralization of the ministry is not to lead to secularism but to a rediscovery of the distinctively Christian understanding of grace and of sacrament.

Edward J. Kilmartin

Although he has not written any single work on the ordained ministry of comparable length to the studies of Cooke, O'Meara, or Tavard, Edward J. Kilmartin, a sacramental theologian and liturgist, has over the last twenty years touched on the theme a number of times and in a variety of contexts. In the course of doing so, he has developed a distinctive and consistent view of the way in which the ministry represents Christ and the church. Important in itself, the issue of representation is a key to much of the contemporary Catholic debate on priesthood and ministry.

Scholastic and post-Tridentine theologians tended to situate priests on the side of Christ over against the church. Christ was seen as mediating his forgiveness and grace to the faithful through the instrumentality of ordained ministers. Building on this theology, twentieth century papal documents formulated the unique relationship of priests to Christ by affirming that in certain acts of their ministry and especially in the eucharist, they act *in persona Christi*. This tradition also recognized that priests represent the church, but this was seen as a secondary representation largely exercised in the non-sacramental parts of the liturgy. Priests represent the church because they first represent Christ who is the head of the church.

For Kilmartin this approach is not only a relatively late development, but it fails to do justice to the liturgical and theological traditions of the first millennium. There the primary reality is the church and not the minister. The Christomonism at the heart of the traditional view is, moreover, quite out of step with recent developments in ecclesiology and pneumatology. The idea of sacrament it presupposes is not that of Vatican II which emphasized the ecclesial nature of all the sacraments and especially of the eucharist. In contemporary Catholic theology, sacraments are not understood simply as acts of Christ through his ministers in the church, but rather as acts of the church itself. They express and celebrate the deepest reality of the church as the body of Christ, the inner life of which is animated by the Spirit. Like Cooke, Kilmartin stresses the risen Christ and his continuing presence to individuals and the church through the gift of his Spirit.

Representing Christ and the Church

Kilmartin, like O'Meara and others, prefers to think of the episcopacy and the presbyterate in terms of pastoral leadership.

Rooted in Christ's own ministry through the historical succession from the apostles, ministers are called forth by the Spirit in order to offer to the community a service of pastoral oversight. It is because they are leaders of the church with a special responsibility for its faith and unity and not because of some sacred power which they have that priests preside at the liturgy.

In this sense the ordained minister directly represents the church and only indirectly Christ and the Spirit who are the source of its life and unity. In a 1977 response to the Vatican declaration on the ordination of women, Kilmartin makes use of the distinction between denotation and connotation. The ritual of ordination and the ministry that flows from it denote the church and its faith while connoting Christ. In liturgical activity, "the priest first represents (denotes) the church in its sacramental activity and secondly represents (connotes) Christ the Head of the Church." As true as this is, Kilmartin also affirms "that from the perspective of what is ultimately signified the priest first represents (connotes) Christ the Head of the Church and secondly represents (denotes) the Church united in faith and love."[3]

As much as Kilmartin insists that ministers represent the church and act in its name, he does not hold that they are simply commissioned by it to do so. The ministry belongs to the essential structures of the church as these were given it by Christ in the Spirit. This is one of the positive implications of the traditional formulation about the minister acting *in persona Christi*. It "correctly stresses that the ordained are not delegates of the community, that their ministry derives from Christ and is supported by Christ and the Spirit."[4] The language is misused when it gives the impression that ministers automatically represent Christ in their ministry or when it is used juridically to justify certain kinds of ecclesiastical obedience.

Central to Kilmartin's position is his insistence that sacraments are acts of worship and that the community is the active subject of their celebration. As expressions of the faith of the church they always entail a prayer to the Spirit. As prayers of the whole church represented in the local community they are inevitably heard. The *ex opere operato* is rooted not in a sacred power of the priest but in the faith of the church.

Although he rejects the traditional idea of the priestly character as a participation in the priesthood of Christ, Kilmartin does not do away with it altogether. It can still be used as a way of affirming that ordination is permanent and can never be repeated, that the ordained person is placed over against the community precisely as serving the faith of the church, and that beyond the minister's personal abilities, he can count on the bestowal of a special gift of the Spirit.[5]

Although Kilmartin prefers to think of the ordained ministry primarily in terms of pastoral office or of leadership, he has no difficulty in applying priestly terminology to it. "As minister of Christ the high priest, and minister of the priestly people, he merits the title priest."[6] The difficulty with this kind of language arises with the claim that the priest participates in the priesthood of Christ. This could lead to the mistaken notion that "the ministerial priest actually participates ontologically in the personal, incommunicable priesthood of the man Jesus Christ."[7] It would be better to say that the priest acts *in persona Christi per Spiritum* or that he participates in the Spirit of the priesthood of Christ.

Christ and the Spirit

Over the years Kilmartin has put a greater emphasis on the Holy Spirit. This may well be a result not only of his liturgical studies but also of his involvement in the Catholic/Orthodox dialogue. Whatever the reason, he stresses that it is in and through the Spirit that the risen Christ is active in the church. A pneumatological ecclesiology not only insists on the indispensable place of the epiclesis or prayer to the Spirit in the sacraments but is sensitive to the phenomenon of charisms. As important as the ordained ministry is to the well-being of the church, it does not exist in isolation. The non-ordained also are the recipients of gifts of the Spirit and these too have to be put at the service of the community. A recognition of the existence and significance of charisms inevitably blurs the line between the proper responsibilities of the ordained and others. This may well be why some recent writers have turned with such enthusiasm to the simplicity and clarity of the traditional Christomonistic approach.

In his major 1988 study *Christian Liturgy,* Kilmartin spells out in some detail the broader liturgical and sacramental background for his understanding of the ordained ministry. The focus is Trinitarian with particular emphasis on the various and interdependent roles of Father, Son, and Spirit in the economy of salvation. The immediate context for the liturgy and thus also for the liturgical leader is ecclesiological. The ministry is seen "as a sacramental representation of the Trinitarian mystery of the Church."[8] It represents Christ, the Spirit, and the church.

"The presiding minister of liturgical celebrations represents the apostolic Church and Christ. By expressing the faith of the Church as formulated in the symbolical language and actions of the liturgy, the minister represents the Church, speaks in the name of the believing Bride of Christ. But the minister also represents Christ in two ways. First, ordained ministers represent Christ in the sense that Christ employs them in his Church to exercise a ministry of leadership by which the community of believers is built up. Second, they represent Christ in the liturgy because they lead the community in worship in the name of Christ. . . . The visible minister, who speaks in the name of the Church, also speaks in the name of Christ, who has missioned the minister to serve as transparency for his operational presence as High Priest of the worshipping community."[9]

Speaking as it does of two different ways in which Christ is represented, this passage seems to give a little more emphasis than earlier articles to this aspect of the minister's role. Later in the same book, however, there is a phrase that hearkens back to what Kilmartin has been saying for twenty years. After affirming that the presiding minister represents Christ, he immediately adds that "he represents Christ because he represents the Church of which Christ is the Head."[10]

What Kilmartin is clearly seeking is a balance between the traditional scholastic position which sees priests primarily as representatives of Christ and recent efforts that so emphasize their relationship to the Church that they become little more than delegates of the community. "The relationship of the liturgical leader to Christ and to the Church must be conceived as one of mutual dependence."[11] The "and" between the two kinds of representation here is not to be understood disjunctively. Both elements belong together and are, finally, inseparable.

Avery Dulles

In his well-known and influential 1974 *Models of the Church,*[12] the Jesuit theologian Avery Dulles developed an approach to ecclesiology that focused on five different and finally complementary "models" that people were using more or less consciously when reflecting on the nature and mission of the church. He described them as: institution, mystical communion, sacrament, herald, and servant. A separate chapter addressed the question of the ordained ministry. His thesis there was as simple as it was illuminating: to each model of the church there corresponds a model of ministry.

In the institutional model the ordained represent a clerical elite responsible for its organization and administration. The mentality is largely juridical. "Priesthood is viewed primarily in terms of power" (163), whether it be the power to rule, to teach, or to administer the sacraments. The communion model, on the other hand, puts a priority on those leadership qualities that are able to deepen a group's community experience and life. The ordained minister must have an ability to work with and inspire others. "The role of the priest . . . is the integration and coordination of all the charisms in a way that serves the unity of the Church." (166)

The language of priesthood is most at home in the sacramental model with its emphasis on liturgy and worship. Through ordination a person is set apart to perform the sacred rituals of the community. It is an office which demands a special holiness, a unique commitment to prayer and religious life. Already in 1974 Dulles saw in Roman Catholicism "a full-scale revolt against the excesses of the sacral concept of ministry." (169) While sympathetic to the rejection of abuses and exaggerations, he was concerned lest the reaction go too far. "Catholicism has perhaps a special responsibility to keep alive the sacral dimension of priesthood." (165)

The herald model puts a premium on preaching and proclamation and tends to think of the minister in terms of the prophetic tradition. Here ordained ministry is primarily ministry to the word. The servant model, on the other hand, demands a ministry that reaches beyond the inner life of the community and that concerns itself with the world and with issues like justice and peace.

Given the variety of models, Dulles felt it unwise to attempt to formulate "a single tight definition of priesthood." The ordained ministry obviously entails a multiplicity of functions all of which no one person could hope to fulfill. Priestly service "may, in particular cases, be more prophetic or more liturgical, more sacral or more secular, more personal or more bureaucratic. . . . The fulness of the priestly office, which very few individuals adequately encompass, would include the building of Christian community, presiding at worship, the proclamation of the word of God and activity for the transformation of secular society in the light of the gospel." (175) The average priest would emphasize one or other of these functions.

A Changed Perspective

Dulles returned to the theme of the ordained ministry in a 1990 talk.[13] The concerns that it reflects and the new emphases in his own understanding of the priesthood that it reveals are indicative of the changing situation of the church over the last twenty years. The paper echoes and is clearly meant to respond to a widespread episcopal and seminary preoccupation with priestly identity.

After a brief overview of his earlier theory of models, he takes up specifically the theme of priesthood, which he understands primarily in a cultic sense. It is this aspect of office that is at the heart of the current crisis. The development from the patristic period through the middle ages to the Council of Trent was certainly in the direction of an ever more cultic and priestly understanding of the ministry and especially of the presbyterate. Against this background, Vatican II marked a careful but genuine shift. It broke out of a narrowly cultic view and included explicitly in its theology of the priestly office pastoral and preaching responsibilities. Its "concept of priesthood, in its full extension, may be said to include not only cultic but also the clerical, the pastoral and the kerygmatic." (286)

In spite of the real gains represented by Vatican II's theology

of ministry, its "doctrine . . . on the priesthood suffers from certain ambiguities that have led to doubts and confusions in the
postconciliar period." (287) The broadening of the notion of priesthood beyond the cultic demanded a rethinking that does not seem
to have taken place. The confusion was related to some degree to
the multiplicity of functions that were now said to be part of the
priestly office. The fact that the council's presentation contained
no clear focus of unity heightened the difficulty.

The pluralism of post-conciliar theology made it unable to
compensate for the council's failure. Theologians developed a variety of theologies of ministry. Some like Rahner and Ratzinger
stressed preaching and the word; others like John Paul II emphasized specifically cultic functions; and still others like Kasper and
O'Meara gave the priority to pastoral leadership. Judging all these
efforts to be one-sidedly preoccupied with functions or tasks,
Dulles offers a synthetic or unitive model which he describes as
"representational." The intention with such a model is to get behind the different functions to "the common source or root from
which they all spring."

The starting point is the notion of the church as sacrament or
representative of Christ. Present in individuals, especially in saints
and in those in need, Christ also makes himself present in the
official acts of the church. "This he does by making certain individuals responsible for the Church's self-manifestation as the body
of Christ and, by that very token, for its corporate fidelity to Christ
its head." (288) Through ordination Christ establishes some members of the church as "his qualified representatives." What is most
distinctive of them is not what they do but what they are in virtue
of ordination. The representational model "penetrates beyond
functionalism to what may be called ontology of priesthood."

The issue of function and/or ontology has been a constant one
since at least Congar's first writings on the priesthood. Dulles'
position has affinities with the interpretation that John Paul II has
given to the phrase *in persona Christi*. It also has parallels with
Kilmartin's use of representative language, although how Dulles
understands the relation among priest, Christ and church is less
clear than in Kilmartin. If the priest is the icon of Christ, his
ministry is markedly ecclesial. The character, for example, is said

to make priests "in a new way ecclesiastical persons—that is to say, public persons in the Church." Although some of the functions that they fulfill can be done by lay people, "when performed by priests they take on, so to speak, greater ecclesial density. They come to be attributable, though in varying measure, to the Church as such." (288)

The sacramental representation of Christ is meant to permeate all that priests do "in the person of Christ as head." Outside the sacraments, however, and "teaching guaranteed by infallibility it cannot be taken for granted that the priest is automatically acting for Christ." There remains a real distance between office and personal holiness. Priests must make a concerted effort if they are to live up to the grace given them, if in all they do they are "to be transparent to Christ."

Concluding Reflections

At the present time there is obviously no single Roman Catholic theology of the ministerial priesthood. This should be neither surprising nor disheartening. The ordained ministry is a rich and many-sided reality, and there are a variety of legitimate approaches to it. What is important in a period of change is that one be open to, and include in one's understanding of it, as many of its elements and aspects as possible.

Catholic theologians need to take the NT data seriously and in a way that pays due respect to modern biblical scholarship. Even as they do so, however, they cannot simply disregard subsequent history. As one-sided as later developments may be, they need to be examined carefully in order to discern the authentic Christian values that may be in them. Some at least of these will have to be integrated into any adequate contemporary theology of ministry. The language of priesthood is a good example. The practice of the NT in this area has to be respected. It points to the radical transformation of priesthood and cult that took place in the person and ministry of Jesus. The very old and very widespread use of priestly terminology in the Catholic tradition, on the other hand, can hardly be abandoned as meaningless. Clearly Christ exercised priestly as well as prophetic and pastoral functions and he continues to do so both in the community as a whole and through its leaders. The challenge is to use the language of priesthood in a way that does not distort or cloud over other aspects of the gospel message.

The ordained ministry cannot be treated in isolation. The community of faith in and for which it exists is endowed with a rich array of gifts of the Spirit including other forms of ministry. A theology of the presbyterate can only be developed within a total ecclesiology, one that is aware both of history and of the challenges and possibilities of the present. Today more than in the past there needs to be a sensitivity to the pneumatological as well as to the christological aspects of both church and ministry. Any effort to play the roles of Christ and the Spirit off against one another will be counterproductive. Church and ministry belong to, and can only be understood within the context of, the one great trinitarian story of salvation.

Attempts to reduce contemporary theological discussions in this area to a contrast between functional and ontological understandings are not, in the end, very helpful. None of the authors cited in the present book holds a "merely" functional view of office. If some of them react in the name of pastoral concerns against an approach that emphasizes a way of life that separates the ordained from the laity, they recognize that ministry is a profoundly religious reality, marked by the gift of the Spirit and demanding genuine holiness of life. A Catholic understanding of ordination as a sacrament includes a recognition that function implies ontology. The word "ministry," on the other hand, reminds the ordained that they have a task to perform, responsibilities to fulfill, a service to offer. It is in relation to this that the ontology of ministry has to be understood.

More work needs to be done on the meaning of the priesthood of religious and especially of those not involved in pastoral ministry. It was a pastoral model that the church inherited from the patristic period and that was stressed at Vatican II. Its rediscovery marks a decisive moment in the renewal of Catholic theology of the ministry, a moment that must neither be forgotten nor repressed. It is not, however, the whole story. The development of active religious communities, one of the most distinctive features of the western church, brought in its wake a new form of the priesthood. This needs to be reappropriated and integrated into a broad theology of ministry, but not in such a way as to make what is an exception the norm.

In the course of history the ministry has taken on a variety of forms. In many cases theology followed practice. The same will be true in the future. The study of history can free the church to be creative in responding to present needs. Some things will have to be tried before it will be known whether they truly are of God or not. Here theology's task will be the humble although important one of recalling basic principles and earlier experiences and of helping to articulate implications of present and proposed pastoral practices.

The writing of the present book has underlined for me again the radical impossibility of reducing the theology of the ministerial priesthood to a few doctrinal statements. The ministry is a religious reality, rooted in the person and teaching of Jesus and nurtured by centuries of Christian experience. It is something that needs to be thought about at some length, prayed over, and, above all, lived out in, with, and at the service of, a concrete community of faith.

Notes

Chapter 2

1. An English translation of MP can be found in *Vatican Council II: More Postconciliar Documents,* ed. A. Flannery (Boston: St Paul Editions, 1982) pp. 672–92. (The date given there should be 1971 and not 1967.)

2. An English translation of the Holy Thursday letters and reflections is available both in pamphlet form and in *Origins* 8 (1979) 696–704; 9 (1980) 655, 657–65; 11 (1982) 704–08; 12 (1983) 687–90; 13 (1984) 751–52; 14 (1985) 696–98; 15 (1986) 685–91; 16 (1987) 792–95; 17 (1988) 737–40; 18 (1989) 729, 731–34; 19 (1990) 748–49. References in the text are to year and to paragraph number.

Chapter 3

1. On Congar see J.-P. Jossua, *Yves Congar: Theology in the Service of God's People* (Chicago: Priory Press, 1968), A. Nichols, *Yves Congar* (London: G. Chapman, 1989), and Y. Congar, *Fifty Years of Catholic Theology,* ed. B. Lauret (London: SCM, 1988).

2. *Jalons pour une théologie du laïcat* (Paris: Editions du Cerf, 1953) was translated as *Lay People in the Church* (Westminster: Newman Press, 1957).

3. Y. Congar, *Sainte Eglise* (Paris: Editions du Cerf, 1963) p. 263.

4. "Un essai de théologie sur le sacerdoce catholique. La thèse de l'abbé Long-Hasselmans: texte et remarques critiques," *Recherches de science religieuse* 25 (1951) 187–99, 270–304.

5. Congar offers an overview of his own changing understanding of priesthood and ministry in "My Pathfindings in the Theology of the Laity and Ministries," *The Jurist* 32 (1972) 169–88.

6. "L'Eglise de Hans Küng," *Revue des sciences philosophiques et théologiques* 63 (1969) 673–706.

7. "Préface" to B.D. Marliangeas, *Clés pour une théologie du ministère: In persona Christi, in persona ecclesiae* (Paris: Beauchesne, 1978) pp. 5–14.

Chapter 4

1. For an introduction to Rahner and to his theology in his own words, see K. Rahner, *I Remember* (New York: Crossroad, 1985) and *Karl Rahner in Dialogue: Conversations and Interviews 1966–1982*, eds. P. Imhof and H. Biallowons (New York: Crossroad, 1986). See also H. Vorgrimler, *Understanding Karl Rahner: An Introduction to His Life and Thought* (New York: Crossroad, 1986).

2. K. Rahner, *The Shape of the Church to Come* (London: SPCK, 1974).

3. K. Rahner, "Priestly Existence," in *Theological Investigations* (TI) III, 239–62.

4. K. Rahner, "Priest and Poet," TI IV, 294–317.

5. See, for example, K. Rahner, "What Is a Sacrament?" TI XIV, 135–48.

6. K. Rahner, "The Meaning of Ecclesiastical Office," in *Servants of the Lord* (Montreal: Palm Publishers, 1968) pp. 13–45.

7. In TI XII, 31–38.

8. My translation; see TI XII, 36.

9. K. Rahner, "Pastoral Ministries and Community Leadership," in TI XIX, 73–86.

10. K. Rahner, "Ignatius of Loyola Speaks to a Modern Jesuit," in K. Rahner and P. Imhof, *Ignatius of Loyola* (London: Collins, 1979), pp.11–38.

Chapter 5

1. For an introduction to Ratzinger and his theology, see A. Nichols, *The Theology of Joseph Ratzinger: An Introductory Study* (Edinburgh: T & T Clark, 1988).

2. J. Ratzinger, *The Open Circle: The Meaning of Christian Brotherhood* (New York: Sheed and Ward, 1966).

3. J. Ratzinger, "Das geistliche Amt und die Einheit der Kirche," in *Das neue Volk Gottes: Entwürfe zur Ekklesiologie* (Düsseldorf: Patmos, 1969) p. 113.

4. J. Ratzinger, "Zur Theologie des Konzils," in *Das neue Volk Gottes,* pp. 147–70.

5. See J. Ratzinger, *Theological Highlights of Vatican II* (New York: Paulist Press, 1966).

6. *Ibid.,* pp. 175ff.

7. J. Ratzinger, "Priestly Ministry—A Search for Meaning," *Emmanuel* 76 (1970) 442–53, 490–505.

8. See his commentary on chapter one of *Gaudium et spes* in *Commentary on the Documents of Vatican II,* ed. H. Vorgrimler (Montreal: Palm, 1969) vol V, pp. 115–63.

9. See "Epilogue: On the State of the Church and Theology Today," in J. Ratzinger, *Principles of Catholic Theology* (San Francisco: Ignatius Press, 1986) pp. 367–93 and *The Ratzinger Report* with V. Messori (San Francisco: Ignatius Press, 1985).

10. J. Ratzinger and H. Maier, *Demokratie in der Kirche: Möglichkeiten, Grenzen, Gefahren* (Limburg: Lahn Verlag, 1970) p. 26.

11. See the three articles brought together in "The Key Question in the Catholic–Protestant Dispute: Tradition and *Successio Apostolica,*" in *Principles of Catholic Theology,* pp. 239–84.

12. *The Ratzinger Report,* p. 56.

13. J. Ratzinger, "Biblical Foundations of Priesthood," *Origins* 20 (1990) 310–14.

14. *Ibid.,* p. 313.

15. J. Ratzinger, *Ministers of Your Joy* (Ann Arbor: Redeemer Books, 1989).

Chapter 6

1. J. Galot, *Theology of the Priesthood* (San Francisco: Ignatius Press, 1985). References to *Priesthood* in this chapter will be by page number in the text.
2. See H. Küng, *Why Priests?* (Garden City: Doubleday, 1972).

Chapter 7

1. On Schillebeeckx and his theology, see J.S. Bowden, *Edward Schillebeeckx: In Search of the Kingdom of God* (New York: Crossroad, 1983) and R.J. Schreiter, "Edward Schillebeeckx: An Orientation to His Thought," in *The Schillebeeckx Reader* ed. R.J. Schreiter (New York: Crossroad, 1984) pp. 1–24.
2. E. Schillebeeckx, *Ministry: Leadership in the Community of Jesus Christ* (New York: Crossroad, 1981).
3. E. Schillebeeckx, *The Church with a Human Face: A New and Expanded Theology of Ministry* (New York: Crossroad, 1985).
4. Galot's review can be found in *Esprit et Vie* 92 (1982) 125.
5. In *Nouvelle Revue Théologique* 104 (1982) 722–38.
6. P. Grelot, *Eglise et ministères: Pour un dialogue critique avec Edward Schillebeeckx* (Paris: Editions du Cerf, 1983).
7. Crouzel's review is in *Nouvelle Revue Théologique* 104 (1982) 738–48.
8. See W. Kasper, "Das kirchliche Amt in der Diskussion," *Theologische Quartalschrift* 163 (1983) 46–53. English translation in *Communio* 10 (1983) 185–95. The reviews of Crouzel, Kasper and Vanhoye were published together in English by the Committee on Doctrine of the US Bishops' Conference, Washington, 1983.
9. In *Revue des sciences philosophiques et théologiques* 66 (1982) 101–05.
10. The CDF's judgment on *Ministry* is in *Origins* 14 (1984) 523, 525.
11. CDF, "The Minister of the Eucharist" (*Sacerdotium ministeriale*), *Origins* 13 (1982) 229, 231–33.
12. For Schillebeeckx's letter, see *Origins* 14 (1984) 526.

13. In *Theologische Quartalschrift* 166 (1986) 156–58.

14. In *Revue des sciences philosophiques et théologiques* 72 (1988) 111–14.

15. The CDF's judgment on *Human Face* is in *Origins* 16 (1986) 344.

16. "Epilogue: La 'Notificatio' du cardinal J. Ratzinger," in E. Schillebeeckx, *Plaidoyer pour le peuple de Dieu* (Paris: Les Editions du Cerf, 1987) pp. 299–304.

Chapter 8

1. Donald Senior, "Biblical Foundations for the Theology of Priesthood," in *Priests: Identity and Ministry,* ed. R.J. Wister (Wilmington: Michael Glazier, 1990) pp. 11–29; here p. 29.

2. J.W. O'Malley, "Priesthood, Ministry and Religious Life: Some Historical and Historiographical Considerations," *Theological Studies* 50 (1989) 527–47; see also his "Diocesan and Religious Models of Priestly Formation: Historical Perspectives," in Wister, *Priests: Identity and Ministry,* pp. 54–70.

3. K. Osborne, *Priesthood: A History of the Ordained Ministry in the Roman Catholic Church* (New York: Paulist, 1988).

4. E. Schüssler Fiorenza, " 'Waiting at Table': A Critical Feminist Theological Reflection on Diakonia," in *Diakonia: Church for the Others,* eds. N. Greinacher and N. Mette, *Concilium* 198 (1988) 84–94; here p. 85.

5. *Ibid.,* p. 89.

6. R.R. Ruether, "Ordination: What is the Problem?" in *Women and Catholic Priesthood: An Expanded Vision,* ed. A.M. Gardiner (New York: Paulist Press, 1976) pp. 30–34; here, p. 33. See also R.R. Ruether, "Guarding the Sanctuary: Sexism and Religion," in *New Women, New Earth: Sexist Ideologies and Human Liberation* (New York: The Seabury Press, 1975) pp. 63–87.

7. R.R. Ruether, "Ordination," p. 34.

8. William Cardinal Baum, "Appendix: A Message on the Priesthood," in *Priests: Identity and Ministry,* ed. R.J. Wister (Wilmington: Michael Glazier, 1990) pp. 149–57; here p. 152.

9. *Ibid.,* p. 142.

10. B. Cooke, *Ministry to Word and Sacrament: History and*

Theology (Philadelphia: Fortress Press, 1976). References to *Ministry* in this chapter will be in the text and by page number only.

Chapter 9

1. G. Tavard, *A Theology for Ministry* (Wilmington: Michael Glazier, 1983). References to this work in this section will be in the text and by page number.

2. T.F. O'Meara, *Theology of Ministry* (New York: Paulist Press, 1983). References to this work in this section will be in the text and by page only.

3. E. J. Kilmartin, "Bishop and Presbyter as Representatives of the Church and Christ," in *Women Priests: A Catholic Commentary on the Vatican Declaration,* eds. L. & A. Swidler (New York: Paulist, 1977) pp. 295–302. The quotation is from p. 299.

4. E.J. Kilmartin, "Office and Charism: Reflections on a New Study of Ministry," *Theological Studies* 38 (1977) p. 553.

5. E.J. Kilmartin, "Apostolic Office: Sacrament of Christ," *Theological Studies* 36 (1975) p. 261.

6. E.J. Kilmartin, "Sacraments as Liturgy of the Church," *Theological Studies* 50 (1989) p. 530.

7. *Ibid.,* p. 531.

8. E.J. Kilmartin, *Christian Liturgy: Theology and Practice,* vol. 1 *Theology* (Kansas City: Sheed and Ward, 1988) p. 196.

9. *Ibid.,* p. 324.

10. *Ibid.,* p. 364.

11. *Ibid.,* p. 325.

12. A. Dulles, *Models of the Church,* expanded edition (Garden City: Image Books, 1983). References to this work in the present section will be in the text and by page only.

13. A. Dulles, "Models for Ministerial Priesthood," *Origins* 20 (1990) 284–89. References to this article in the present section will be in the text and by page only.

Bibliography

Congar, Y., *Lay People in the Church* (Westminster: Newman Press, 1957)

——, *Power and Poverty in the Church* (Baltimore: Helicon 1964)

——, *Priest and Layman* (London: Darton, 1967)

——, *Ministères et communion ecclésiale* (Paris: Editions du Cerf, 1971)

——, "Le sacerdoce du NT: mission et culte," in *Les Prêtres,* eds. Y. Congar and J. Frisquet (Paris: Editions du Cerf, 1968)

——, "Quelques problèmes touchant les ministères," *Nouvelle Revue Théologique* 93 (1971) 785–800

——, "Sur la trilogie: prophète—roi—prêtre," *Revue des sciences philosophiques et théologiques* 67 (1983) 97–116

Cooke, B., *Ministry to Word and Sacrament: History and Theology* (Philadelphia: Fortress Press, 1976)

Dulles, A., *Models of the Church,* expanded edition (Garden City: Image Books, 1983)

——, "Models for Ministerial Priesthood," *Origins* 20 (1990) 284–89

Galot, J., *Theology of the Priesthood* (San Francisco: Ignatius Press, 1985)

Kilmartin, E.J., *Church, Eucharist and Priesthood: A Theological Commentary on 'The Mystery and Worship of the Most Holy Eucharist'* (New York: Paulist Press, 1981)

———, *Christian Liturgy, Theology and Practice,* vol. 1, *Theology* (Kansas City: Sheed and Ward, 1988)

———, "Apostolic Office: Sacrament of Christ," *Theological Studies* 36 (1975) 243–64

———, "Office and Charism: Reflections on a New Study of Ministry," *Theological Studies* 38 (1977) 547–54

———, "Pastoral Office and the Eucharist," in *Bread from Heaven* ed. P. Bernier (New York: Paulist Press, 1977) pp. 138–50

———, "Bishop and Presbyter as Representatives of the Church and Christ," in *Women Priests: A Catholic Commentary on the Vatican Declaration,* eds. L. & A. Swidler (New York: Paulist Press, 1977) pp. 295–302

———, "Lay Participation in the Apostolate of the Hierarchy," in *Official Ministry in a New Age,* ed. J.H. Provost (Washington: Canon Law Society of America, 1981) pp. 89–116

———, "Ecclesiastical Office, Power and Spirit," *Catholic Theological Society of America Proceedings* 37 (1982) 98–108

———, "Sacraments as Liturgy of the Church," *Theological Studies* 50 (1989) 527–47

O'Malley, J.W., "Priesthood, Ministry, and Religious Life: Some Historical and Historiographical Considerations," *Theological Studies* 49 (1988) 223–57

O'Meara, T.F., *Theology of Ministry* (New York: Paulist Press, 1983)

Osborne, K., *Priesthood: A History of the Ordained Ministry in the Roman Catholic Church* (New York: Paulist, 1988)

Rahner, K., *Servants of the Lord* (New York: Herder & Herder, 1968)

———, *Theology of Pastoral Action* (New York: Herder & Herder, 1968)

———, *The Priesthood* (New York: Herder & Herder, 1973)

———, *The Shape of the Church to Come* (London: SPCK, 1974)

———, "Priestly Existence," in *Theological Investigations* III (New York: The Seabury Press, 1967) pp. 239–62. Other relevant articles of Rahner can be found in *Theological Investigations,* vols. IV, VI, XII, XIV, XIX

Ratzinger, J., *The Open Circle: The Meaning of Christian Brotherhood* (New York: Sheed and Ward, 1966)

————, *Principles of Catholic Theology* (San Francisco: Ignatius Press, 1987)

————, *Ministers of Your Joy* (Ann Arbor: Redeemer Books, 1989)

————, "Priestly Ministry—A Search for Its Meaning," *Emmanuel* 76 (1970) 442–53, 490–505

————, "Biblical Foundations of Priesthood," *Origins* 20 (1990) 310–14

————, with V. Messori, *The Ratzinger Report* (San Francisco: Ignatius Press, 1985)

Ruether, R.R., "Guarding the Sanctuary: Sexism and Ministry," in *New Women, New Earth: Sexist Ideologies and Human Liberation* (New York: The Seabury Press, 1975) pp. 63–87

————, "Ordination: What is the Problem?" in *Women and Catholic Priesthood: An Expanded Vision,* ed. A.M. Gardiner (New York: Paulist Press, 1976) pp. 30–34

Schillebeeckx, E., *Ministry: Leadership in the Community of Jesus Christ* (New York: Crossroad, 1981)

————, *The Church with a Human Face: A New and Expanded Theology of Ministry* (New York: Crossroad, 1985)

Schüssler Fiorenza, E., " 'Waiting at Table': A Critical Feminist Theological Reflection on Diakonia," in *Diakonia: Church for the Others,* eds. N. Greinacher and N. Mette, *Concilium* 198, (1988) 84–94

Tavard, G.H., *A Theology for Ministry* (Wilmington: Michael Glazier, 1983)

Wister, R.J., ed., *Priests: Identity and Ministry* (Wilmington: Michael Glazier, 1990)

Other Books in this Series

What are they saying about Salvation?
by Rev. Denis Edwards
What are they saying about God and Evil?
by Barry L. Whitney
What are they saying about Mark?
by Frank J. Matera
What are they saying about Luke?
by Mark Allan Powell
What are they saying about Social Sin?
by Mark O'Keefe, O.S.B.
What are they saying about John?
by Gerard S. Sloyan
What are they saying about Acts?
by Mark Allan Powell